To the children of Bailey's Elementary School for teaching me
what it means to be a mathematician

Numbers

I like the generosity of numbers.
The way, for example,
they are willing to count
anything or anyone:
two pickles, one door to the room,
eight dancers dressed as swans.

I like the domesticity of addition—
add two cups of milk and stir—
the sense of plenty: six plums
on the ground, three more
falling from the tree.

And multiplication's school
of fish times fish,
whose silver bodies breed
beneath the shadow of a boat.

Even subtraction is never loss,
just addition somewhere else:
five sparrows take away two,
the two in someone else's
garden now.

There's an amplitude to long division,
as it opens Chinese take-out
box by paper box,
inside every folded cookie
a new fortune.

And I never fail to be surprised
by the gift of an odd remainder,
footloose at the end:
forty-seven divided by eleven equals four,
with three remaining.

Three boys beyond their mothers' call,
two Italians off to the sea,
one sock that isn't anywhere you look.

—*Mary Cornish*

Contents

Foreword

THE FOCUS ON EARLY EDUCATION IN THIS COUNTRY has been primarily on language arts, especially on reading and writing. Much has been written about how to use reading and writing workshops in the elementary classroom. But another equally important subject that individuals need to function in our society is mathematics. While we all can agree that math is important, there are few books that help teachers learn how to use math workshops in instruction. That is, until Kassia Omohundro Wedekind's *Math Exchanges* came along.

Teaching mathematics well to young children is challenging. How do we use children's prior knowledge and understanding to develop instruction? How do we develop math communities of learners where the thinking, questions, and interests of students are valued? And finally, how do we engage young children in discussions of substance with each other and their teachers? The publication of *Math Exchanges* remarkably improves the prospects for elementary teachers to implement math workshops that focus on "community, rigor, and joy"—math workshops where there is an exchange of ideas that address the important questions mentioned above. *Math Exchanges* offers teachers a grounded approach, supported by research and professional knowledge, to designing and implementing math workshops that help develop young mathematicians. In the math workshops described in this book, students actively construct their understanding of a particular topic, such as grouping numbers by tens, and then come together in small groups—known as math exchanges—to share ideas and reflect on what they understand or have accomplished during whole-class lessons and independent work. Kassia Omohundro Wedekind shares with us valuable and practical ways to teach mathematics using math workshops and, in particular, math exchanges in kindergarten through grade three.

Kassia is a teacher and math coach with a great deal of experience helping young students and colleagues make sense of mathematics. In this delightful book she introduces us to methods of interaction in which students are treated as mathematicians involved in inquiry. Through thoughtful classroom vignettes, Kassia shares ways to conduct math exchanges. She describes problem-solving math exchanges by elaborating on different problem types and structures. She has done what is needed in professional books for teachers—linked research to practice—and she has done it in a way that makes the material accessible, interesting, and motivating.

There are a number of chapters in *Math Exchanges* that the reader will want to refer to again and again. One is Chapter 3, on planning, where Kassia emphasizes the purposeful planning of math exchanges. The chapter gives detailed explanations of how she decides what mathematics to introduce to students and how students might make sense of the topic or problem. More important, I appreciated reading about how Kassia reflects on what a student's use of different strategies tells her, as the teacher, about his or her understanding. Another chapter readers will want to refer to multiple times is Chapter 8, "Reflection and Self-Monitoring." The importance of reflection and articulation of thinking is well known, and their impact on our teaching cannot be emphasized enough. Finally, the appendix is chock-full of useful material, such as monthly organizational charts and recording sheets for analyzing student work, so that teachers can apply what they have learned to their own classrooms as they begin to implement math exchanges.

Teachers will learn a great deal about teaching and learning mathematics by reading *Math Exchanges*. They also will be, at times, in awe of the work and ideas that kindergartners (see Chapter 6!) and first, second, and third graders are capable of producing. I am so glad that Kassia took the time to share her thoughts and experiences at Bailey's Elementary School by writing this book.

Suzanne H. Chapin

Acknowledgments

THIS BOOK IS FIRST AND FOREMOST a Bailey's book. I thank my lucky stars that I ended up teaching (and learning!) at Bailey's Elementary School in Fairfax County, Virginia. I may have been the person to sit down and write this book, but it was crafted and created by many phenomenal teachers and students. Thank you for letting me be a part of your stories and share them with the rest of the world! These teachers include Tricia Brown, Mary Anne Buckley, Kathleen Fay, Melissa Fleischer, Michelle Gale, Debbie Gates, Mimi Granados, Margaret Hall, Christy Hermann, Katie Keier, Rachel Knieling, Elizabeth Levine, Phoebe Markle, Steve Miner, Lauren Nye, Jessica Shumway, and Suzanne Whaley. Thank you also to the kindergarten and second-grade teams for sharing your teaching lives with me for the past two years.

An amazing school needs amazing leadership. I'm lucky always to have worked with wonderful administrators who stand up for what is right in public education.

Anyone who knows me knows my groupie-like devotion to the many great thinkers of the math and literacy education worlds. This book would not be complete without a sincere thank-you to Catherine Fosnot and Maarten Dolk. I turn to *Young Mathematicians at Work* again and again for inspiration and guidance. I also turn to the wise words of Mary Cowhey, Thomas Carpenter, Susan Empson, Elizabeth Fennema, Megan Franke, Peter Johnston, Ellin Keene, Linda Levi, Debbie Miller, and Regie Routman for their clear and powerful voices on education.

Thank you to Nina Liu, who read my chapters as I wrote them and whose thoughtful insight and advice made this book much richer than it would have been without her.

When you sit down one day and decide to write a book, chances are you will need lots of guidance, support, honest critique, and chocolate chip cookies. I certainly did! I am blessed to live and work within a five-mile radius of some of the greatest educators and writers out there. One of these people is Pat Johnson, who happens to write at the same Panera as I do! Pat read and offered her thoughts on every chapter of this book (and sometimes on several versions of a single chapter!). I am truly fortunate to have such an amazing mentor and friend. And how many first-time authors get e-mails from their mentors that say, "It's Saturday morning. I'm at Panera. Where are you? Shouldn't you be writing?" I'm lucky to be one of the many to know Pat Johnson as "Aunt Pat."

As a collector of quotes, one of my favorites is from C. S. Lewis, who said that "friendship is born at that moment when one person says to another, 'What! You too? I thought I was the only one.'" My friends keep me from being "the only one" every day. Katie, I met you on my first day at Bailey's. Since then I've learned many things from you, the two most important being how to be a passionate and compassionate teacher and how to be a true friend. I couldn't imagine a life—or even a day—without you, my friend. Christy, someone as reflective, deeply caring, and hysterically funny as you are is a rare gem. Thank you for letting me share and learn from you and your students. And thank you for teaching me that when you arrive at a yoga retreat on the side of the mountain with no yoga mat, you should laugh and carry on. A true yogi needs no mat. Carol, my friend, we have shared many laughs, tears, and chicken paninis together. Thank you for showing me through your example and advice that it is possible to be a wonderful teacher and writer and also be human. Tricia, our daily 7:00 a.m. phone calls on the way to school keep me going day after day. You inspire me with your commitment to your students and your loyalty to your friends. And perhaps most of all, thank you for being someone I can laugh with until I gasp for air. And to Katy, my best friend forever. From the apple orchards to the top of Tikal to the sacred burial grounds of Santa Fe, you have been there as a true friend. I'm looking forward to many more adventures together soon and for many, many years to come.

Thank you to my mom and dad for believing in me and for being proud of me every step of the way. For my mom who tells all of her friends I am the world's best teacher (it's nice to have that unwavering support!) and for my dad who called every weekend to check on how the book writing was going. I love you both. And thank you to Aunt Dottie for being the teacher in our family who inspired me.

Toby Gordon, my editor, supported me throughout the writing of this book. I don't know how she did it, but she always knew what question to ask to get me thinking, when to push me on further and when to let me ponder something for a while. Thank you, Toby, for believing in me and this book, even on days when I did not. Thank you to Erin Trainer and Jay Kilburn for the great care and expertise you brought to the making of this book. Thank you, also, to everyone at Stenhouse for your guidance and for allowing me to join the Stenhouse family of authors.

And, of course, thank you to Aron, my sweet husband. I'm lucky to share life and laughter with you. Thank you for encouraging me to go out there and do the work that I'm most passionate about and for always believing I can do it. Here's to wide open weekends, my love!

Creating Space for Math Workshop

The life of a mathematician is dominated by curiosity, a desire bor-
dering on passion to solve the problems he is studying.

—Jean Dieudonné

MATH WORKSHOP, AT ITS BEST, is passionate and fiery. It hums with life as children inquire, discover, create and re-create meaning, and connect their ideas
with those of the world around them. Does this sound different from your experiences learning math? I know it does for me! My own memories of learning
math are of time spent completing boring worksheets, memorizing procedures that would help me pass tests, and an overall feeling of disdain toward
the subject. When I became a teacher of mathematics, I knew this was not what
I wanted for my students, but I had no idea how to teach math differently.

When I began teaching at Bailey's Elementary School, a diverse Title I
school just outside of Washington, D.C., in Fairfax County, Virginia, where
students come from over forty different countries and speak over twenty different languages at home, I knew that I needed to teach in a different way
than I had previously. As I began to explore and figure out what I wanted to

do differently as a math teacher—how I wanted students to learn, and how I wanted to teach—I drew upon what I knew about reading and writing workshops. Although much has been written about establishing strong reading and writing workshops, few books have focused on the importance of the math workshop. Over the years as a classroom teacher and now as a math coach, I have had the opportunity to experiment with the parallels in creating a reading and writing workshop community and creating a math workshop community. In creating math workshops, my greatest inspiration often has come from the literacy world.

In *Teaching Essentials*, Regie Routman writes about reading and writing workshop. She writes about "inviting everyone into the learning community" and holding high expectations for all—even, and perhaps especially so, for those children who have been officially or unofficially labeled by their perceived deficits rather than their capabilities (2008, 4). Community, rigor, and joy are at the heart of the workshop approach to teaching and learning. As literacy teachers, many of us have worked hard to define and establish this kind of workshop community. Nancie Atwell, in *In the Middle* (1998), writes about reading and writing workshop as a space in which choice, a sense of ownership, time to think deeply, strong community, and responsive teaching are the foundations of instruction and learning.

Envision a workshop as a space for learning in which the learners become the leaders. Slowly but surely, responsibility is transferred from the teacher to the children. They become self-directed, motivated, and independent. They take risks, challenge themselves, and monitor their own learning. Although it is the teacher who initially establishes the workshop environment, it is the children who create the community. Their interests, ideas, questions, struggles, and achievements serve as the teacher's guide and the foundation of the workshop.

Debbie Miller, in *Teaching with Intention* (2008), describes walking into a reading workshop:

> *I see kids gathered around tables, desks, and rugs on the floor, reading and interacting in a variety of authentic ways to picture books, poetry, chapter books, magazines, nonfiction, and more. They're working independently, with partners, and in small groups. I hear the buzz of conversation and collaboration. Almost everywhere I look I see evidence of rigorous, joyful learning . . . "Hey! Where's the teacher?" I suddenly wonder. It dawns on me that in the midst of falling in love, curious kids, and walls that talk, I'm not even sure she's in the room. And then I spot her, seated next to a child, eye-to-eye, conferring . . . No one is looking*

at the clock; there's not a hint of rush. There's simply the luscious feeling of endless time. (10, 13)

So what do these wonderful ideas about reading and writing workshop have to do with math? Some of our greatest ideas and convictions about teaching and learning in reading and writing workshop have the power to change how we view the teaching and learning of mathematics. We can make a shift from mathematics as something we simply "do" to a way in which we live our lives, relate to each other, and wonder about our world. We can create, for our students, these spaces for exploration and discovery in a place we call math workshop.

Math Workshop at Bailey's Elementary School: A Structural Framework

Over the past few years, Bailey's Elementary School has been working to create and put into practice what we call "Essential Elements of Math Workshop." This structural framework, described in the following sections, is our attempt to break down the common components of math workshop throughout grades K–5 while acknowledging the diverse ways in which math workshop may be implemented within this general framework. The framework, in other words, offers a starting point for teachers implementing math workshop. It offers teachers entry points into significant conversations about both instruction and student work within math workshop.

The Opening

(Usually 5–10 minutes)

The opening of the math workshop is the first opportunity to engage the whole class in mathematical thinking that relates to the workshop focus. Students gather in a group on the rug (or in chairs, for older students) as a community of mathematicians. The opening of the workshop may take the form of a daily routine, group problem solving, math vocabulary development, or the sharing of parts of our mathematical lives with one another. The opening might also focus on a certain mathematical statement about behaviors of mathematicians (such as "Mathematicians make predictions and estimations") that the teacher is encouraging children to engage in during the day's workshop.

Focus Lesson

(Usually 10–20 minutes)

The focus lesson sets the mathematical focus for the day. The lesson is always tied to a specific math standard and launches students into an exploration of that concept. Teachers draw focus lesson content from state and national standards, textbooks, supplemental math resource books, and their own ideas. This is a time for the whole group to share ideas and for mathematicians at different levels of understanding to exchange ideas, strategies, and thoughts.

Independent Practice

(Usually 30–40 minutes while the teacher works with small groups)

Depending on the structural format teachers choose for their math workshop, students work individually, in pairs, or in small groups on mathematical tasks, games, and story problems. They work independently from the teacher, but not from each other; they usually work in pairs or with a small group. What this looks like varies from class to class (see Figures 1.1 and 1.2). Some teachers use a center-based approach in which small groups of students work collaboratively, rotating from task to task after a certain amount of time decided upon by the teacher. In this format, each small group usually rotates through a teacher-facilitated center that focuses on the needs of that particular group of students. Other teachers offer a menu of options for students to choose from, while still others prefer that all children work individually on the same open-ended task. The most important aspect of this element of the math workshop is that it be both truly independent and mathematically meaningful.

Small-Group Math Meetings, or Math Exchanges

(Usually 30–40 minutes; concurrent with independent practice)

During the small-group meeting part of math workshop, which I refer to as math exchanges, teachers work with small groups of children to help expand their understanding of the big ideas of mathematics (see Figure 1.3). The teacher's focus is on guiding student talk and mediating thinking as students share problem-solving strategies, discuss how math works, and move toward more effective and efficient strategies and greater mathematical understanding.

The rest of the chapters in this book focus mainly on work with students during math exchanges.

Figure 1.1 Kindergartners work in pairs to play a math game with Unifix cubes.

Figure 1.2 Third graders work together in a small group on a geometry task during independent practice time.

Figure 1.3
Third graders
discuss their
problem-solving
strategies in a math
exchange.

Reflection

(Usually 5–10 minutes)

Although often the shortest part of the math workshop, reflection has the power to be one of the richest. Group reflection offers time for students to share ideas they discovered during the math workshop (see Figure 1.4), ask questions of each other, argue their points, and solidify their understanding. This time also offers a chance for the teacher to check in with students after they have spent time on their own during independent practice time, especially if they didn't meet with the teacher that day for small-group work.

Figure 1.4
Josue shares his work and thinking during reflection time.

Core Practices of Math Workshop

So, how does this kind of math workshop differ from that of a more traditional math class? In *To Understand: New Horizons in Reading Comprehension* (2008), Ellin Keene outlines "a climate of rigor, inquiry, and intimacy" as a crucial part of literacy learning (32). Similarly, I believe that there are core practices among strong math workshops that promote such a climate of joyful rigor, inquiry, and intimacy. These ideas go beyond the structure of the math workshop format and delve into what math workshop is all about.

Promoting a Climate of Rigor, Inquiry, and Intimacy

As you reflect on what you want math workshop to look like, sound like, and feel like in your own classroom, this outline of the role of the teacher and the student in the math community may be helpful:

Teachers	Students
Identify themselves as mathematicians who are continually growing and learning	See teachers not as the source of all mathematical knowledge but as fellow mathematicians who are continuing to learn both inside and outside the workshop
Believe that all students are powerful mathematicians and treat them as such	Identify themselves as mathematicians who have valuable ideas to contribute to the field of mathematics
Create a predictable daily math workshop structure in which there is extended time for independent and collaborative exploration and application of mathematical ideas	Take responsibility for the independent and collaborative choices they make that will promote growth as mathematicians; feel a sense of purpose in their work
Facilitate learning and coach learners rather than view learners as "empty slates" to be written upon	View peers as valuable resources for greater mathematical understanding; view teachers as sources of mathematical collaboration rather than just the source of the "correct answer"
Teach important concepts in depth over a significant amount of time	Explore and apply important concepts throughout the math curriculum

(continued)

(continued)

Teachers	Students
Create time for small-group math exchanges, time in which groups of diverse mathematicians gather to problem solve collaboratively	Work with peers to understand, experiment with, and apply a variety of problem-solving strategies, and identify effective and efficient strategies
Present rich, contextually authentic problem solving to students	Realize the usefulness of math and extend their knowledge of and interest in math beyond the confines of the workshop
Create a culture of joyful rigor	Challenge themselves, take risks, and explore their own questions and wonderings
Facilitate rich reflection among students through discussion, sharing student work, and creating visual anchors of student thinking to which children and teachers can refer and which serve as footprints of learning	Understand, engage in, and grow from the collective work of the mathematical community

Recently, in my role as a math coach, I sat down to chat with some teachers who were interested in implementing math workshop. All of these teachers wanted to build a strong community of mathematicians who asked questions, learned from one another, and understood math as more than a set of rules and procedures to memorize. They shared some of their worries about starting math workshop:

"I just don't know where to start."

"How will I know what to teach?"

"This sounds great, but we don't have the time to let students discover and construct meaning for themselves. There are too many standards to teach them!"

"Can I still use parts of the textbook?"

"What are the other kids doing while I work with small groups?"

"How will I have time to plan for all of these small groups?"

"How will I know if my students are learning?"

"It seems overwhelming."

Listening to them, I realized that these were the exact same thoughts I had when I first started teaching math workshop! Strong teachers, like the ones with whom I was talking, are always questioning their teaching methods and wondering how to improve their practice. There is no "right" way to do math workshop. There is no one system that works for everyone. Math workshop is much more than a framework of how we spend our daily math instructional time. Yet strong math workshops do share a philosophical foundation that drives instructional decisions.

Theoretical and Philosophical Foundations of Math Workshop

When I first began teaching math I fully believed that if I only *explained* a concept clearly enough and provided enough engaging experiences to reinforce the math skills I was teaching, all of my students would learn. For quite a while I operated under this behaviorist framework that asserted that the role of the teacher is to "preplan a curriculum by breaking a content area . . . into assumed component parts—'skills'—and then sequence these parts into a hierarchy ranging from simple to more complex" (Fosnot 2005, 9). This made sense to me. After all, this is how I learned math and how my textbook, math program, and state standards were designed.

It took me a while to realize that this approach simply wasn't working for all of my learners and did not support the development of strong mathematicians. Sure, some students learned the math skills I presented and did well on tests, but many did not. And more importantly, I could not even begin to claim that my students truly understood math.

In math workshop, learning occurs when children are actively engaged in their environment and work to create a system of meaning and deep understanding. Within this framework of learning and teaching, teachers are not the guardians of knowledge whose job it is to pass down information held sacred and untouchable under the rules that govern math. Quite the contrary. It is the role of the students to "raise their own questions, generate their own hypotheses and model possibilities, test them out for viability, and defend and discuss them in communities" (Fosnot 2005, 34). The role of the teachers is to provide problem-solving experiences that invite questions, wonderings, and space for grappling with new thinking that may cause children to rethink their previous ideas about how math works. Teachers of math workshop facilitate this construction of knowledge and guide students toward greater understanding in which skills are embedded, but not isolated.

Humans as Mathematicians

Part of the beauty of mathematics is how uniquely and universally human it is. Humans are born mathematicians. Recent research has shown that humans are born with (or at least develop within the first few months of life) the foundations of numeracy, specifically, an understanding of quantity. Although many compelling experiments have supported this idea, one that I find particularly fascinating is that of American researcher Prentice Starkey, whose research is described by Devlin (2005).

Starkey's subjects, babies between six and eight months, were shown a collection of two objects and a collection of three objects simultaneously projected on two side-by-side screens. As the collections of both two and three objects were shown simultaneously on the screens, a recording of either two or three drumbeats would play. Using video equipment and analysis of the amount of time the babies spent looking at the projections of two or three objects, Starkey's experiment showed that when two drum-beats were played, babies spent significantly more time looking at whichever screen was showing a collection of two objects at that moment. Similarly, when three drumbeats were played, the babies spent significantly more time looking at the projection of the collection of three objects. Starkey's research shows that even very young children have a sense of number (Devlin 2005).

Devlin (2005) also describes the discoveries researcher Karen Wynn made. In Wynn's experiment, babies sat on their mothers' laps in front of an empty puppet theater and a camera that recorded the infants' facial reactions. Hidden from view behind the puppet theater, the experimenter placed one puppet on the stage. The experimenter then placed another puppet on the stage. Next, a screen was raised to hide the puppets. Then the screen was lowered so that both puppets were visible to the baby.

The experimenters repeated this performance several times. However, the show was sometimes varied at the point when the screen was lowered to reveal only one puppet or to reveal three puppets. Analysis of the amount of time spent staring at the puppets revealed that babies spent, on average, one second longer staring at the puppets when one puppet or three puppets were revealed. Wynn concluded that, after initially seeing two puppets on the stage, the babies expected to see two puppets when the screen was lowered. They were surprised when the outcome of placing one puppet and then another puppet on the stage did not result in two puppets in all.

Wynn's research was so surprising that it was challenged by many in the scientific community. Nevertheless, subsequent experiments similar to that of Wynn all led to the same conclusion. Babies have a sense of numerosity—demonstrated by their ability to recognize changes in the size of collections up to three objects (Devlin 2005).

So, what are the implications of such research? Why should we care that babies seem be able to identify and distinguish between quantities up to three? As a society, we interact with math in a detached manner. We accept the learning of mathematics to be a pragmatic necessity. We believe children should have a certain mastery of math concepts. But, I wonder, how many of us consider mathematics to be a fundamental part of who we are as humans?

The research of Starkey, Wynn, and many others suggests that math, rather than simply being a human construct built out of necessity, is in fact a part of our most basic make-up as humans. If that is true, why do so many of us and so many of the children we teach struggle to make sense of mathematics? If we are indeed born mathematicians, how can we create a more organic understanding of math and the teaching of mathematics?

Children as Mathematicians

When people visit my classroom, one question I am often asked is why I refer to my students as mathematicians. When most people imagine mathematicians, they imagine professional adult mathematicians. However, I believe this is a very limited definition that hinders both children and adults from achieving a sense of mathematical self-efficacy. Peter Johnston devotes his book *Choice Words: How Our Language Affects Children's Learning* (2004) to illustrating how the specific language we use with our students can tremendously influence how they see themselves, their classroom community, and the world. In describing how children construct identities as readers, Johnston writes, "Children in our classrooms are *becoming* literate. They are not simply learning the skills of literacy. They are developing personal and social identities—uniqueness and affiliations that define the people they see themselves becoming" (22).

In order to achieve a deep and true understanding of mathematics, children must first see themselves as becoming mathematicians. They must identify themselves as mathematicians, take on the responsibility of learning to do the work of a mathematician, and make meaning of their world through mathematics.

Mathematician Statements: Constructing Our Identities as Mathematicians

Perhaps the most important philosophical underpinning of math workshop is that all children and teachers view themselves as mathematicians. Viewing oneself as a mathematical thinker is just as crucial to the teaching and

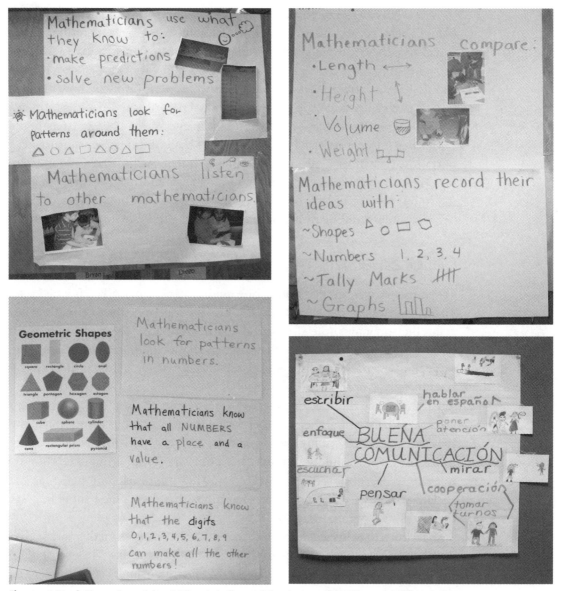

Figures 1.5a–d The mathematician statements in Figures 1.5a–d were created in several different classes.

learning of mathematics as viewing oneself as a reader and writer is to the teaching and learning of reading and writing. Part of the way we can help students construct their identities as mathematicians is through the use of mathematician statements (see Figures 1.5a–d). Just as we spend significant time exploring what readers and writers do we must also spend time with our students understanding just what it is that mathematicians do.

Fosnot and Dolk (2001) use the term *mathematize* to explain the process by which children (and their teachers!) use mathematics as one lens through which to understand and construct meaning in our world. They write that "children, in learning to mathematize their world, will come to see mathematics as the living discipline it is, with themselves a part of the creative, constructive mathematical community, hard at work" (13).

Mathematician statements can be introduced and practiced through any kind of mathematical content. It is often helpful to make charts of mathematician statements that include student-generated examples, drawings, and photos of your community of mathematicians at work that serve as anchors and reminders of the important work of mathematicians.

Mathematician statements (I use the phrase "what mathematicians do" when working with students), like standards, help us focus and guide our instruction. Throughout this book, I will introduce mathematician statements relevant to the material being discussed. Some mathematician statements are related to the building of mathematical identity and community, while others are focused on specific content understanding and processes.

Some of the mathematician statements were created by my own second- and third-grade communities. Others were developed by the first-grade team of teachers at Bailey's Elementary School during some of their shared math meeting time. Others still are adapted from the National Council of Teachers of Mathematics' process standards (NCTM 2011a). You may find some of these statements useful for your own mathematical community. You may come up with your own statements that reflect the values and practice of your math workshop. And I can almost guarantee that the best mathematician statements you will use will come from your students (see Figure 1.6).

The following are some mathematician statements that are specific to the questions "Who are mathematicians?" and "How do they work?" These kinds of process-oriented statements can be taught at various points throughout the year when you see a certain need in your community, or they may be ideas that come from your students as they embrace ownership over the math workshop.

We Are All Mathematicians: Identity-Building Statements

- Mathematicians are curious. (When my class focuses on this statement, we always study Albert Einstein and his great quote, "I have no special talents, I am only passionately curious.")
- Mathematicians ask themselves questions.
- Mathematicians need lots of time to think, think, think.

- Mathematicians look for challenging problems in their world to figure out.
- Mathematicians persevere.
- Mathematicians make lots of mistakes, but they keep on thinking.
- Mathematicians change their ideas and strategies and come up with new ones. Then they change their ideas again. This is part of being a mathematician.
- Mathematicians talk to and question other mathematicians in order to help themselves understand.
- Mathematicians do not always agree! Disagreeing respectfully is part of being a mathematician.
- Mathematicians work together. They explain their ideas and thinking. They listen to the thinking of other mathematicians.

Mathematician statements such as these get at the core of what being a mathematical thinker is all about. These statements help us connect the specific content we are teaching with the bigger idea of what math is and what mathematicians do.

Some of this construction of a mathematical identity initially comes from the teacher. From the first day of school, I set the tone for the ongoing definition of our community and individual mathematical identities. "Mathematicians look for challenges to figure out," I often say to my class of third graders as I encourage them to stick with tasks that at first may seem too difficult or overwhelming. "Mathematicians work with and talk to other mathematicians to help themselves understand," I say when I am teaching the children how to listen deeply and respond to the thoughts of their fellow classmates. It's not long before the children begin to take over the role of defining their identities as mathematicians.

"Mathematicians make a lot of mistakes, but they keep on thinking," Melanie once told me as I watched her and a group of other kids struggling with figuring out how to approach a problem-solving situation.

"That's so true, Melanie," I respond, delighted. "Let's talk about that during our reflection with the whole class later. I think that might be an important idea to write and put up in our room to keep thinking about."

Even very young children can take on and craft identities as mathematicians. About a month after the school year started, I was working on a story problem with two kindergartners, William and Hannah. After I had told the two little mathematicians a story about pigs escaping from a farm, William jumped right into modeling the problem with tiny toy pigs and drawing his ideas on paper. Hannah sat contemplatively. "Do you want me to tell you the story again, Hannah?" I asked, thinking she had not understood the story.

"No," she replied. "Sometimes mathematicians just need time to think." Indeed they do, Hannah!

Making our beliefs about the process of mathematics and the work of mathematicians explicit to our students is an important part of the workshop philosophy. In order to build a community of mathematicians, we must spend time constructing the identity and work of individual mathematicians and a mathematical community as a whole; this work necessitates a combination of both planned and spontaneous moments.

A Glimpse into Math Workshops

Let's take a peek into a few classrooms at Bailey's Elementary to see what math workshops look like in practice. If you're like me, you need to be able to imagine what a practice looks like, sounds like, and feels like before you can begin to understand and implement something new.

The following three math workshops look fairly different on the outside. The names of the workshop parts vary a bit from classroom to classroom. The children in these classrooms are different ages, the classes focus on different math content, and we see them at different points throughout the school year. Math workshops are diverse. Yet notice how these three communities have common ground in their individual and group identities as mathematicians.

Michelle's Kindergarten Math Workshop

Routines: 10–15 minutes
Centers/Small-Group Work: 30–40 minutes
Reflection: 10–15 minutes

It is late September in Michelle Gale's kindergarten classroom. Michelle's class starts the day with math. They begin by sitting in a circle together talking about the day's math routine. Today, Michelle's routine, the Counting Jar, comes from the *Investigations in Number, Data, and Space* curriculum series (TERC 2008). "Let's look at what is inside the Counting Jar today," says Michelle to her kindergartners. Michelle dumps out the Counting Jar, revealing four candy corn and three candy pumpkins. "Who can count up the candies today?" There is no shortage of volunteers willing to count and organize the candy.

Vera is first. She carefully arranges the candies in a line and then touches each candy as she says, "One, 2, 3, 4, 5, 6, 7."

Juan is next. He separates the candy corn and pumpkins into two groups. "One, two, three, four," he says, touching each candy corn. "One, two, three," he continues, counting each pumpkin candy. Juan pauses and looks up at Michelle, not sure what to do next.

"So, how many candies altogether?" asks Michelle.

Juan looks back to the candies and recounts all of them from one. "Seven!" he exclaims. "Same as Vera said."

"Oh, so a group of four and a group of three is the same as seven," comments Michelle.

As several students finish their turns organizing and counting the candy, Michelle asks them, "So, how many are there?" to confirm their knowledge of cardinality, the concept that the last number we say when counting and touching objects is the total. Michelle then turns to the class. "Mathematicians have different ways of organizing to help them count. How did Vera and Juan organize and count the candies?"

After Michelle's students discuss strategies for organizing the counting of the candies, they use counting notebooks to represent the number of candies and write the numeral 7. Some children represent the seven candies immediately by drawing and writing in their notebooks. Other children gather other collections, such as shells, stones, beans, and other counters that Michelle keeps in tubs near the circle. These children count out seven objects and then represent them in their notebooks through drawing and writing. Still others represent seven with circles or tally marks.

After her Counting Jar routine, Michelle quickly reviews some centers in which the children will be working. Many of the centers Michelle uses correspond with the *Investigations in Number, Data, and Space* curriculum. Other centers focus on open-ended exploration of manipulatives and number-writing practice. While in some centers the students work independently, students in other centers may require Michelle's instructional assistant to help coach them through their task.

Michelle also uses the time children are working in centers to meet with small groups focusing on counting tasks and story problems.

At the end of her sixty-minute math workshop, Michelle gathers the children in their circle again to revisit the idea of sorting, organizing, and counting with a purpose. Although the counting reflection is very similar to the Counting Jar routine, children are constantly coming up with new ideas and refining their strategies. Today Michelle dumps some pumpkins and gourds from a bag and asks children to take turns organizing and counting them. Michelle returns to some of the same questions she asked in the Counting Jar routine, while also asking the group, "How does Amyr sort and organize the pumpkins and gourds? Does it help him figure out how many there are?"

"I know!" yells Cruz. "There are still seven like the candies. But it's not four and three. Now Amyr organized with five orange pumpkins and two white gourds."

"And it's still seven again," confirms Amyr.

Christy's First-Grade Math Workshop

Calendar Routines: 10–15 minutes during morning meeting
Focus Lesson: 15–20 minutes
Centers: 30 minutes (one center per day)
Reflection: 5–10 minutes

"As you're working in your centers today, you're going to be thinking about something that mathematicians do," first-grade teacher Christy Hermann says as her kids transition from the focus lesson on using pan balances to explore equality and inequality to working in centers.

Christy pulls out a chart, and the class reads the mathematician statement they have been focusing on for a couple of weeks. "Mathematicians use what they know to make predictions and estimates," they read together.

Christy's centers this week are designed around her mathematician statement. In the math tools station, students are working with pan balances. They sort through a basket of odds and ends and make predictions about the weight of these objects before testing their predictions of equality or inequality with the pan balances.

Another center, puzzles, relates to problem solving. From the outside, this center may look like these kids are "just playing puzzles," but listening to them, we see that they're really developing spatial problem-solving skills that are the foundation of much of mathematics. Most of the children are actively talking about their predictions.

"Aha! I thought that green piece would go with the other tree pieces, and it did!" Aria proudly declares.

As Christy's class rotates through this center throughout the week, some of the first graders sort puzzle pieces by shape or color before assembling the puzzles, whereas others assemble the outside edges of the puzzle first. A few argue about where to go next with their difficult puzzle, but the ideas exchanged in their passionate conversation show how Christy has set up her math workshop to promote just this kind of authentic, meaningful discussion.

At the computer station, students are playing math games that encourage numerical estimations. Christy has used past whole-group focus lessons to teach these games and to model her own prediction and estimation think-alouds in an effort to make sure students stay meaningfully engaged so that the computer center does not become just a "guessing game." Her work has paid off. Even though every student in the computer center has his or her own computer, they often go back and forth between each other's screens to offer help, opinions, and ideas.

Meanwhile, Christy sits down at a table with a small group. She starts by giving the children five minutes of practice that she has pulled from the *Investigations* student workbook. As students complete this skill practice, which they have learned how to do independently and cooperatively, Christy checks in on the other centers, making sure that all the children are engaged.

When Christy returns to her small group, the kids quickly compare ideas on their worksheets before moving on to the story problems, which they will focus on for the next 25 minutes or so.

Because Christy's math workshop is set up so that students spend about 30 minutes in one center and complete one center per day, these first graders have developed the necessary stamina to delve into more complex problem solving when they are working with Christy, as well as maintain authentic, meaningful work when in their center groups.

As center time comes to a close, Christy rings a chime. "Strike a pose!" she says with a smile, and the kids stop working to strike a silly pose. She rings the chime again, "Strike another pose!" She has the kids' attention now, and this brief physical activity helps reenergize them. "Let's clean up and come to the circle to reflect about our predictions and estimates."

Back in the reflection circle, Christy points back to the chart paper. "We're sharing how you made predictions and estimates, and how those worked out."

Savanna, who had been working in the pan balance center, shares her prediction. "I thought the crayon would be equal to the button, but the crayon was down. [The side of the pan balance with the crayon was lower, thus proving it was heavier.] I knew I had to add another button to make it equal. I was wrong, but I made another prediction and it was right." This may sound like a simple observation, but Savanna has just made a big jump in her thinking about equality. While Savanna had previously searched for two individual items that were equal in weight, on this day she discovered that two of one kind of item (buttons, in this case) could be equal to one of another kind of item (one crayon).

"So," comments Christy, "it sounds like you used what you learned from testing your first prediction to help you make a new prediction. That's what we're trying to do as mathematicians."

Many other students chime in with questions for Savanna. "Did you try the scissors? They weighed a lot. Probably more than ten crayons!" Much of the conversation goes back and forth between the students, rather than only between the student sharing and the teacher. Christy has spent a lot of time focusing on teaching children to listen and respond to each other. When one student shares, Christy often asks another child to restate that child's idea before adding a comment or question. Although this reflection time may last only five minutes, students often come out of it with deeper understanding and more questions and ideas to try out.

Kassia's Third-Grade Math Workshop

Routines: 10–15 minutes
Tasks and Small-Group Work: 30–40 minutes
Reflection: 10–15 minutes

As we come in from recess, my wonderfully rowdy and out-of-breath students pile onto the carpet in front of a large whiteboard. "Circle or clump?" asks Erik, referring to the different arrangements we use for our opening routines.

"Let's use a circle today," I tell the kids as they peel off their coats, drink from the water fountain, and come to the rug. I want all of us to be able to see each other and the ideas we'll write on the board.

"Let's do some counting by hundreds today. We're not going to start at 0 though. Let's start at 1,799 and count forward by hundreds."

Counting around the room is one of the regular routines with which the students are comfortable (see Figure 1.7). In the beginning of the year we counted by twos, fives, tens, hundreds, and thousands starting from zero and then starting from other numbers. I usually record the numbers on paper, a number line, or number grid as students count orally. We have spent considerable time analyzing patterns of change as we count by different numbers and thinking about how our counting can help us solve math problems.

"Whoa! Take a look at that number!" shouts Erik, who does much of his processing aloud. He starts counting to himself quietly and scooting closer to the easel of chart paper.

"Aha!" I think. "He is taking on the challenge."

Figure 1.7
A small group of second graders counts around the circle.

"Before we start counting," I say, "I want you to make an estimate. If we count this way and count all around the circle, what number will the last person say?"

Students look around. They know we have twenty-three kids in our class. Some are checking to see if anyone is absent. Some are wondering if it will be more or less than 1,000 more than our starting number of 1,799. After giving them a moment to think, I record a few estimates from the students, always following up with, "Why do you think that?"

"I think our last number will be 2,799," offers Harrison, "because that's 1,000 more than where we started."

"No, I think it's more than that," adds Emilio. He's unsure and looks around the class to see if others will agree with him.

"Why do you think that, Emilio?" I probe.

"I know!" yells out Melanie.

"Okay, Melanie, let's listen to Emilio's idea and see if it matches what you're thinking," I say.

"Well, if we're counting by 100, 1,000 more would be ten people who count a number. See, 100, 200, 300, 400, 500, 600, 700, 800, 900, 1,000. Ten people," Emilio says, holding up the fingers he has used to track the ten groups of 100 that are equal to 1,000.

"What do you think, Melanie?"

"I agree. We have more than ten people here. So, I think maybe we need to add 2,000 more to 1,799."

"What would that be, Cecilia?" I ask, trying to pull one of my quiet, anxious students into the group conversation.

She looks up into the air for about thirty seconds. The class gives her "thinking time," as we have practiced. "Three thousand seven hundred ninety-nine," Cecilia says firmly.

"Okay, let's write that down as an estimate," I say. We could continue on with estimates, but I feel like this is a good place to stop and start the counting practice.

As each student adds his or her number to our count, I record the number on the whiteboard. After we've counted we look back at our numbers. I often ask questions like, "What changed as we counted? What stayed the same? What happened after Isey said 1,999?"

After our opening, we break into partners I have established for the week. The pairs begin by independently solving a story problem I have designed to go with our counting routine:

In the morning Rafa put on his pedometer. He knows a healthy person should take 10,000 steps per day. By 11:00 a.m. Rafa has taken 4,499 steps. How many more steps does he need to take today to make his goal of 10,000 steps?

Students are familiar with the context in this problem. We've been playing around with pedometers at recess and when we walk from place to place within our school. They've already been thinking informally about exactly how much activity is necessary for a person to take 10,000 steps in a day. "I bet we'd all be a lot healthier with two recesses," one of my smart mathematicians commented to me after recess one day when he realized that he still needed over 5,000 more steps to reach his goal.

After students have taken time to solve the problem independently, I hear them sharing their strategies and ideas with their partners. We've practiced this kind of sharing a lot. Children are not satisfied just because they have the same answer as their partner. They listen carefully. I hear them saying, "I don't understand what you did in this part," and one student tells her partner, "Oh, I could have done jumps of 1,000 instead of 100. That would have taken a lot less time."

As students are immersed in their problem solving, I call a group of four or five students to work with me. As I start chatting with my group, I check the other students who are working on their independent practice out of the corner of my eye. They check the choice board as they finish the problem-solving task and move on to another task or game of their choice. Some of the choices are familiar ones that we have practiced many times, and one or two choices are new this week, but we have learned and practiced them as a group. Some choices are designed by students' own interests. When I look around I see that some students have chosen a subtraction game that focuses on using a number line to represent one's thinking. Others are writing their own story problems.

A few students are exploring some work we have been doing with growing patterns and geometric blocks. "Look," says Jorge. "We can make something that looks like a bike with these blocks. The circles can be the wheels. When we start it can be a regular bike with two wheels. Then we can say that every day we add a new wheel, and ask, 'How many wheels will the bike have after 10 days, 20 days, 100 days, and 200 days?'"

"Oh that's a good one! So on the tenth day it would be ten extra wheels and the two you started with," I hear Jorge's partner say as they go off to collect blocks and paper for recording.

What I should mention here is that five minutes prior to Jorge's great enthusiasm for his growing pattern he was sitting in a corner refusing to get started on his independent learning time. Jorge is a child who often shuts down when he anticipates potential challenges. I usually check in with Jorge as he makes his choice from the choice board. We read the choices together, and he usually chooses a task we have practiced many times and with which he feels he can be successful. The workshop allows Jorge to make choices (within the limitations of the choice board); he is able to move past his comfort zone and challenge himself independently, while feeling successful with his process and product.

As math workshop draws to a close for the day, students clean up and come to the circle for reflection time. Like Christy's class, we have been working on the mathematician statement, "Mathematicians use what they know to make predictions and estimates." I see Cameron listen carefully as Melanie explains how she made several estimates on a pedometer problem.

"First, I didn't really understand the problem, so my estimate was 2,000. Then I suddenly realized that 4,499 is kind of close to 5,000 and I know that 5,000 plus 5,000 is the same as 10,000, so 5,000 was a better estimate."

Melanie sighs, satisfied. She has said all this in one big breath of a sentence. I look around, wondering if anyone understood how she changed her estimates as she worked through the problem to work toward a more reasonable estimate without focusing on getting the exact answer.

Cameron is looking thoughtful. "What are you thinking about what Melanie said, Cameron?" I ask.

"I think next week we should write, 'Mathematicians change their ideas as they think.'"

"Yes!" I think to myself.

"What do the rest of you think?" I say, turning the conversation back to the class. "Why do you think Melanie's estimates made Cameron think of this new mathematician idea?"

❖❖❖

Just as with reading and writing workshops, these three math workshops echo and reaffirm the importance of time to think deeply, choice, a sense of ownership, a strong community, and responsive teaching.

Why Math Workshop?

Math workshop certainly is not the easiest path to take. We have plenty of outside resources willing to tell us exactly what, when, and how to teach our students. And yet, none of those resources has the intimate knowledge of your community of mathematicians that you have. Math workshop communities create empowered learners—both students and teachers—who question, wonder, explore, and make conjectures. Rigorous joy in math is within the realm of the possible—it is, in fact, what makes math workshop worth it! As you implement math workshop in your classroom you will, no doubt, notice many positive changes and outcomes, some of which are collected in the list that follows.

Outcomes of Math Workshop

- Students experience joyful rigor.
- Students see math as flexible and learn many strategies for approaching problems.
- Because choice is a critical part of math workshop, students take ownership over their learning, knowing that their conjectures, investigations, and strategies are the foundation of the workshop.
- Students view peers as valuable mathematical resources with whom they can collaborate and from whom they can learn.
- Students learn to engage in rich discussion of strategies and ideas and value the learning process over a single correct answer.
- Students see problem solving as a challenge. They persevere through difficulty and do not define themselves by failure if they do not reach a correct solution.
- Students learn to self-manage and self-monitor through independent and group work. They begin the process of taking responsibility for their own learning.
- The role of the teacher is expanded to that of facilitator and coach.

2

Math Exchanges: From Students to Mathematicians

JOHN STEINBECK WROTE, "As happens sometimes, a moment settled and hovered and remained for much more than a moment. And sound stopped and movement stopped for much, much more than a moment" (1994 [1937], 91). This is what we are striving for every day as we work with children— meaningful moments that will "hover" and develop in the minds of young mathematicians, that will take on a deeper meaning beyond the moment in which they occur.

Defining and Building Math Exchanges

When I first thought about and established some core beliefs about teaching math, I knew I needed to think more critically about how I was working with small groups of children. No longer could I view our time together as a place to reteach, rehash, or remediate concepts previously taught to the whole class. If I were to truly live and practice my beliefs about mathematics and

25

mathematicians, I knew I needed to change how I viewed the purpose of small-group work, and thus how I worked with small groups of mathematicians.

Math exchanges, the term I use to define the space, place, and time in which teachers work with small groups of young mathematicians, are spaces that nurture joy, rigor, and empowerment and inform the other parts of our math workshops. Mathematicians are created inside and outside of the math workshop, but there is something special about the closeness of working with a few mathematicians to tackle a problem. If we believe that learning math is much more than learning a series of operations and procedures, then the way in which we work with small groups of children must reflect this as well. Math exchanges focus on building number sense and a deep understanding of the big ideas of mathematics, but perhaps most importantly, math exchanges help nurture young mathematicians who will construct their own definitions of, beliefs about, and purposes for math.

As with all journeys, there are few shortcuts or quick fixes and no magic formulas or scripted narratives for success for math exchanges. I offer no glossy promises. I do, however, invite you to share in a process in which there are many joys, frustrations, and ongoing experiments. I offer you a place beside me as a fellow learner in which we will question, doubt, and spend time pouring over student work, wondering what the next step will be for each child. We will work to become experts on the development of each of our young mathematicians. We will facilitate deep growth and under-standing. This is the work of a math exchange. It is a space to embrace the unknown, to inquire, to play, to work, to struggle, and to learn and relearn.

Understanding the Work of Math Exchanges

One spring afternoon as my third graders transitioned from the whole-group focus lesson into working independently during math workshop, I asked Marta, Evangeline, Herman, and Alex over to the round table to examine a praying mantis egg sac we found during an exploration of our school's court-yard the previous day. "Oh!" Alex shouted. "This is the thing we found out-side yesterday with those bugs inside."

"Yep, this is an egg sac where the praying mantis laid her eggs," I responded, pausing for a moment to let them all touch the egg sac and talk about it.

"Yeah, we found three of those egg sacs outside yesterday!" added Evangeline.

"All hidden in those bushes. I didn't even know what they were before!" Herman followed up.

"Well, neither did I," I reminded them. "Remember? We had to ask Mrs. Rosenbaum [our school's outdoor science teacher] what they were. Yesterday after school I saw Mrs. Rosenbaum again, and she told me something else about the egg sacs that I think you all will really be interested in. She told me that the baby praying mantises won't hatch until the summer, but when they do, up to about 400 little praying mantises can come out of this one little egg sac!"

"Wow! That's a lot!" Marta said with a surprised laugh. We were all completely involved in the moment. The voices and sounds from the rest of the children, working independently and with partners on problem-solving tasks, had faded into the background.

"Today I have a story problem for you about these praying mantis egg sacs," I continued. "Evangeline, you reminded us that we found three egg sacs outside yesterday. We know they won't hatch until the summer, but today we're going to imagine how many praying mantises *could* hatch from the egg sacs. Let's read this story first without the numbers, and see what we can figure out."

I handed each child a piece of paper with the story written on it and blanks where we would write the numbers I'd selected for this group (see Figure 2.1). At the top of the page were pictures of the praying mantis sacs that we took the day before in our outdoor exploration. The four young mathematicians each grabbed one of our special, colored problem-solving pens we use only during math exchanges. Unlike many math classes, we use only pens during math workshop. I teach the children to draw a single line through something if they change their ideas instead of scribbling it out beyond recognition. "All of our thinking is important," I tell them, "even if we change our ideas and answers along the way." As a teacher, having children use pens allows me to view the footprints of their thinking and not just their final answer or idea.

Let's reflect for a moment on the bigger idea of what is happening in small moments such as the one I just described. Someone asked me recently why I use the term *math exchange* to describe working with small groups of students. "Kassia, isn't what you're doing just the same as small-group math?" The answer is yes . . . and no.

Small-group math instruction has traditionally been seen as a form of reaching children who struggle to understand. When I first began teaching math, I, too, thought that if only I could pull all these struggling students

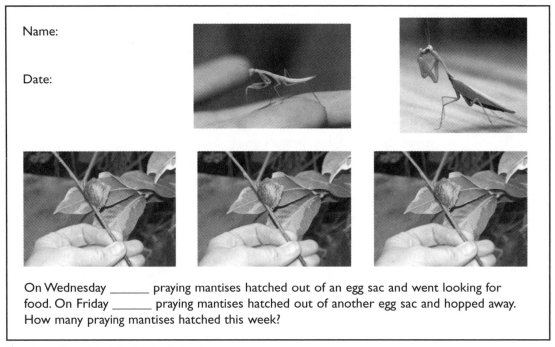

Name:

Date:

On Wednesday _____ praying mantises hatched out of an egg sac and went looking for food. On Friday _____ praying mantises hatched out of another egg sac and hopped away. How many praying mantises hatched this week?

Figure 2.1 Our Praying Mantis Story Problem

together in a small group I could teach something again, differently, in a better way—that if I only worked hard enough I could *make* these students understand. My intentions were good—but this kind of instruction does not work. Both my struggling students and I ended up frustrated. I ended up doing more and more of the thinking for them in order to *make* them understand at the pace and level where I so desperately wanted them to be. However, when these struggling kids left the small group they went right back to being confused. Our work together had not produced any real change in their thinking.

I knew this kind of small-group instruction was not serving my students' best interests or aligning with my beliefs about teaching math. And so I began the journey of working toward a different kind of small-group math instruction—one that builds deep understanding over time and helps students build on what they know, constructing new meaning and understanding through their interactions with peers and the guidance of the teacher.

There is no single "right" way to work effectively with small groups of mathematicians, but these threads are common to successful math exchanges:

1. Short, focused sessions that bring all mathematical minds together
2. Content and context that are responsive to the needs of the specific group of mathematicians
3. Meaningful guided reflection

Many teachers, even those comfortable with teaching math, struggle to implement meaningful, consistent small-group work within their math workshop format. This book is about understanding the power of math exchanges and finding effective ways to make them work within your classroom. We teach in a time of ever-increasing standardization, and many times the unique role of the classroom teacher to understand and be responsive to each individual child's needs is lost in the search for one program, textbook, or pacing guide that will "solve" everything and everyone in one fell swoop. Regardless of the math program or curriculum you are using, working to understand each individual child's math development and how to responsively guide children to deeper understanding through small-group work remains the strongest way in which we, as teachers, can promote a strong mathematical foundation for our learners.

Much of the philosophy behind teaching and learning through math exchanges comes from the work of those who developed Cognitively Guided Instruction (CGI). In *Children's Mathematics* (1999), Thomas P. Carpenter and his coauthors explain CGI as a philosophy that asserts that "children enter school with a great deal of informal or intuitive knowledge of mathematics that can serve as the basis for developing understanding" of mathematics (4). A classroom rooted in CGI philosophy uses problem solving as the main vehicle of mathematics instruction and understanding. The problem types and development of strategies described in *Children's Mathematics* and the other publications by the developers of CGI are an invaluable resource to any teacher who is working to implement this philosophy through small-group math exchanges.

Also critical to our role as teachers in guiding young mathematicians is understanding how children construct the set of interconnected ideas that form the basis of number sense and the big ideas of mathematics. Catherine Fosnot and Maarten Dolk, in their book *Young Mathematicians at Work* (2001; one book in a series), refer to this as the "landscape of learning comprising the big ideas, strategies, and models" (163). Fosnot and Dolk describe "the landmarks the students pass (collectively and severally) in their journey through this landscape that inform teachers' questions, instructional decisions, and the curriculum" (163). Each student's journey toward mathematical understanding is different, but to teach effectively it is essential to understand how children's ideas develop.

As a teacher, I want children to build an interconnected system of ideas and understanding of math, to work together to problem solve, and to build a community of learners who see math not just as a set of useful skills, but as a creative and useful process. By implementing math exchanges into my math workshop, I have been able to do that. Before we return to the small group working through the praying mantis problem, let's think a little about how groups like this one are formed.

Coming Together: Forming Groups That Make Sense

Groups for math exchanges are flexible. Every time I plan a new group meeting, I choose specific children to be in the group for specific reasons. Children do not remain with an identified "math group" for the entire school year. The groups are *responsive* to a specific need. Children need to interact with all kinds of mathematicians. The idea of grouping kids by ability level is counterproductive to the idea that mathematicians learn from each other. Regie Routman sums up this idea perfectly when she asserts that when readers are grouped by ability, "low-performing students are deprived of the benefits of thinking and discussing with higher-performing peers" (2008, 78). The same is true of mathematics; children should be grouped by their mathematical needs, which can be entirely different than their "ability level."

Although *flexible grouping* has come to be a popular term in education, it is often used to describe grouping that is anything but flexible. Often the "flexible grouping" of children for whole-group and small-group instruction is only a euphemism for ability grouping. Perhaps there are assessments given along the way, and a few children move from group to group, but the great majority of children remain classified by the old crippling practice of separating "those of us who are good at math" from "the rest of us."

So how *should* we form groups for math exchanges? I was reminded of the importance of this question after a teacher came into my room when I was working with a group of students. Later she casually remarked to me, "I was so surprised you put *those* kids together."

Those kids were Alex, Marta, Evangeline, and Herman, the four third graders I wrote about earlier in this chapter, who were preparing to do some problem solving related to praying mantises. Upon first glance, these four may seem like an odd group. Marta is a very strong mathematician who knows how to articulate her solid mathematical understanding. She enjoys attempting and talking about interesting problem-solving tasks that challenge her, even if she isn't able to solve them immediately. Evangeline also embraces challenges but has many fewer tools and less efficient strategies than Marta has. Alex is impulsive. He is eager to take on a task but often loses stamina and interest at the point of difficulty. Herman, in looking for "quick tricks" to solve problems, often tries to use traditional algorithms he only partially understands. As a result, Herman is often unsure whether his ideas and answers make sense. Given a traditional assessment, the scores of these four kids would be all over the map. Despite their apparent differences in mathematical understanding and skills, I chose this group with a specific purpose in mind. I wanted these four students to practice listening to and talking about a specific strategy used by a member of the group, and to work to understand why he or she had chosen it. I wanted the child explaining the strategy to work to justify the use of this strategy for this particular problem.

Let's return to the children working through the praying mantis problem with me. I watched them finishing up the problem solving. Herman was rereading the story problem: "On Wednesday 397 praying mantises hatched out of an egg sac and went looking for food. On Friday 205 praying mantises hatched out of another egg sac and hopped away. How many praying mantises hatched this week?"

I chose the numbers in this problem carefully. During whole-group discussions with the class, some students had begun explaining their ideas using compensation strategies. We had talked about how mathematicians examine the numbers in a problem and base their choice of strategy on efficiency for the particular problem and numbers. In this problem I chose the number 397 because of its proximity to 400. As the students began to work on the problem, I wondered if they would notice this and use it to help them solve the problem efficiently. Of these four students, I had seen Marta and Evangeline use compensation strategies in their work previously. Evangeline had used compensation only with smaller numbers. Marta was comfortable with executing compensation strategies, but I wondered if she could clearly explain *why* they worked.

I watched quietly as the group made sense of the problem. Alex and Herman worked together, carefully constructing the numbers with base ten blocks. Herman took the lead. "Alex, you make 205 and I'll make 397. Then we can see how many praying mantises there were. You know, we'll put them all together." Evangeline had been watching them quietly but hadn't written anything yet.

"What are you thinking, Evangeline?" I asked.

"I'm just thinking that it's a lot of work to make all that with blocks."

"Oh. And are you thinking that there is an easier way to do it?"

"Well, 397 is close to 400, so you could just build it with four hundreds blocks," Evangeline responded.

"But it's *not* 400, it's 397. That's different," responded Alex, satisfied with his strategy.

Marta had already solved the problem using a compensation strategy. On her paper she had written:

$$397 + 3 = 400$$
$$400 + 205 = 605$$
$$605 - 3 = 602$$

Having quickly solved the problem, Marta sat back and considered what the others were building with the base ten blocks. Evangeline, seemingly stumped by what to do once she had changed 397 to 400, solved the problem using her tried-and-true strategy of decomposing the numbers in order to add them according to their place value, a valuable strategy but not the most efficient for this problem. She wrote:

$$397 + 205 =$$
$$300 + 200 = 500$$
$$90 + 0 = 90$$
$$7 + 5 = 12$$
$$90 + 12 = 102$$
$$500 + 102 = 602$$

By this time, Alex and Herman had finished constructing and combining the numbers with base ten blocks. All four students arrived at the correct answer. In this case, I was fairly confident they would each have a strategy that would get them there. However, their strategies could not have been more different in terms of both understanding the math and efficiency of computation. I could have stopped the work there. We'd all arrived at an answer of 602. I could have been satisfied. But this would not have been a math exchange. No change had occurred in the minds of the four young mathematicians.

I carefully crafted my words. "Let's take a look at Marta's strategy. She solved the problem a little differently, but I think there's a connection to what

Evangeline was thinking about with the number 400, and I'm wondering if we can show Marta's strategy using the tools Herman and Alex chose for this problem, the base ten blocks."

Our discussion continued for the next five minutes. Marta explained her strategy, and Evangeline was able to retell it, making the jump to why it was possible to change 397 to 400 if you "made up for it" at the end of the problem by subtracting three. Marta and Evangeline helped Alex and Herman construct the compensation strategy with the base ten blocks. "Four hundred is a lot easier to build. It's just a little bit more than 397," commented Alex. The four mathematicians were all at different points in understanding the strategy I'd hoped to highlight with this problem. And that was okay. My goal for this math exchange was not for everyone to solve 397 + 205 using a compensation strategy. My goal was for students to consider and work to understand the efficiency of problem-solving strategies based on the kind of problem and the numbers they were solving.

Although there are sometimes "aha" moments within a single math exchange that produce great and lasting change within the mind of a child, in most cases true change occurs over time. When someone brings up a compensation strategy at another point during math workshop, Herman might remember that this is similar to what we discussed in the praying mantis problem math exchange. A few days later when adding 49 + 22, Alex or Evangeline might try solving the problem using 50 + 21. Marta's experience explaining her strategy might clarify her thoughts and allow her to continue developing a wide range of sophisticated problem solving for different problems and numbers. The power of math exchanges is in the changes they produce over time.

Math exchanges emphasize *change*. This may sound simple, but the purpose of meeting with small groups of mathematicians is to produce change and growth in their thinking. Too often, teachers meet with groups for the sake of meeting ("It's time to pull these five kids together! What should we talk about?") and without a specific focus. They may have the vague notion that meeting with small groups of mathematicians (or perhaps only meeting with struggling mathematicians) is a good practice. Math exchanges put the focus on planned, purposeful exchanges between mathematicians of different abilities.

I chose those four mathematicians with a purpose, knowing that they would approach the problem with different background knowledge and strategies for solving it. This was exactly what I wanted! Through questioning—by me and other members of group—and conversation, my goal of having these children work to explain and justify more efficient strategies was achieved. As I watched them work and bump into issues of efficiency of problem solving, I guided the conversation toward a discussion of how their different strategies took into account this important concept of efficiency. That doesn't mean that the next time these students encounter this kind of problem-solving situation all of them will all be able or will choose to use such efficient strategies. However, the seeds for deeper understanding have been planted. They have owned the work done in this group session, to which I will now be able to refer as we continue developing and refining our ideas throughout the math workshop.

Nudging the Exchange Toward the Big Ideas

Part of building a strong mathematical community is finding the balance between process and product. When I begin a new school year with students unfamiliar with math exchanges, there is often a tendency among children to focus exclusively on getting the right answer through any means necessary. Our first math exchanges sound a little like this:

"I got twenty-six."

"Yep, the answer is twenty-six!"

"Twenty-six? Me, too. That's right."

"It's twenty-six, Ms. Wedekind. We're done. So, what do we do now?"

Of course, they are a little thrown off when I follow with questions like, "Are you sure?" and "How do you know?" My goal is not to diminish their confidence or enthusiasm for solving a problem correctly but rather to nudge them toward ideas that go beyond the fact that the answer is, indeed, twenty-six.

At my school, like many others, we teach the children to explain their answers, to show their work, and to justify their answers to their peers. Our goal is for students to successfully solve problems while also considering new ideas, strategies, and patterns emerging as they solve. One of the goals of math exchanges is to help children make connections between what they know and what they are just beginning to learn. I choose each problem with a purpose—with an idea of what I want students to discover or build upon. This is something that cannot be accomplished if I allow students to see problem solving as dealing with a string of unrelated problems that we want to hurry up and solve in order to get to the next, more difficult problem.

Luckily, children have some of the most adaptable and incredible mathematical minds out there. Before long, kids have moved on from "Listen, lady, the answer is twenty-six. I know I'm right, now let's all move on" to a deeper level of reflection that sounds more like this:

"Look, when we add ten to sixteen, we get twenty-six. The tens place changes, but the six stays the same."

"That's like when I added thirty-four plus ten. I thought I had to count up with my fingers, but then I remembered a pattern. When you add ten, the tens place changes, but the ones place always stays the same."

And of course, as their teacher I will still always have questions: "That's an interesting pattern you are noticing. Does that always work? How could we test that idea out?"

You've seen how I try to balance process and product in my math exchanges. Let's take a look at a couple of math exchanges across different grade levels to see other teachers balancing process and product while also nudging students toward the big ideas behind the problems.

Katie Keier, a first-grade teacher, sits on the floor with four of her students, who all have a whiteboard in front of them that they are using for problem solving today. Katie has just asked them to solve 10 + 7. A couple of them immediately write down *17*. Others count on from 10 using their fingers to keep track of when to stop. "So we agree that 10 plus 7 is 17," says Katie. "Now I'm going to give you another problem. Think about if 10 plus 7 can help you with our next problem, 9 plus 7." A couple of children use the same counting-on strategy they used with 10 + 7, not seeing any real similarity between the problems that can help them. A couple of students, though, immediately write down *16* on their whiteboards. This is the big idea Katie hoped this group would bump up against. As Katie proceeds to guide the conversation, she'll point out that while everyone got the answer of 16, some kids used derived facts or a compensation strategy to quickly solve 9 + 7 mentally.

"Abdel, how did you solve nine plus seven in your mind? Did ten plus seven help you?" asks Katie.

"Well," explains Abdel, "I already know 10 plus 7 is 17. Nine is 1 less than 10, so the answer to 9 plus 7 will be 1 less than 17. That's 16."

Katie checks in with a couple of other kids in the group to see if they understand what Abdel is thinking. Rebecca responds, "Abdel knows that 10 plus 7 is 17 just like 10 plus 6 is 16 and 10 plus 8 is 18. It's a pattern, so he didn't have to count." It looks like most of the children are making a connection to the plus-10 facts but don't yet understand the connection between plus-10 and plus-9.

"Oh, so that is how Abdel solved that first problem so quickly. Let's write down those facts we know with ten on the chart paper and then see if we can figure out how that helps us when we add numbers to nine."

After the kids have helped Katie construct the chart, they return to looking for patterns and connections between plus-10 and plus-9 facts.

Rachel Knieling's second-grade class has been focusing on problem solving with fractions. Today a group of children sit with Rachel working on this problem:

Four kids want to share five pancakes so that every kid gets the same amount of pancake. How many pancakes can each kid eat?

In planning for this math exchange, Rachel wanted to know what her small group of students would do with the "extra" fifth pancake. Would they share the pancake equally among the four friends? Would they know the notation $\frac{1}{4}$?

Rachel watches her students working with the problem. They all begin by drawing the five pancakes and four stick figure people, but what they do from that point varies. One student ignores the extra fifth pancake. Another divides the extra pancake into four unequal parts. A couple of students draw a model of four people, each with their whole pancake and one quarter of a pancake, but have not yet figured out the notation of $\frac{1}{4}$. Rachel knows her next move is a discussion with the group about what to do with this extra pancake and a return to the question of how many pancakes each kid can eat.

As students and teachers become more comfortable in the math exchange environment, more meaningful conversations arise. The teacher becomes better at identifying the important ideas around which to center the conversations, and kids become better questioners and wonderers rather than just students in pursuit of the right answer.

The Time Issue: Frequency and Consistency of Math Exchanges

Every teacher I know struggles with issues of time. There is never enough of this precious commodity. In *Teaching Essentials*, Regie Routman writes about "teaching with a sense of urgency." Before reading her words, I had always associated urgency with a feeling of anxiety. However, after reading and thinking further I found that "the expectation that there is not a minute to lose, that every moment must be used for purposeful instruction" rings true not just within the context of teaching literacy, which Routman writes about, but throughout our entire day as teachers (2008, 96).

Time Within Each Math Exchange

Although I do not set hard-and-fast rules for the length of math exchanges, I have found that the most powerful math exchanges are usually between ten and twenty minutes, depending on the age of the mathematicians and the purpose of the group. Kindergarten math exchanges may last only five minutes. This gives the group enough time to retell and talk together about the meaning of the problem-solving work, attempt the task, and listen to and reflect on the strategies of different group members (see Figure 2.2).

When I first began to experiment with math exchanges, I found that I often became so immersed in the ideas of one particular group that I would look up at the clock and realize I had spent thirty minutes with that one group of four students. I knew I wanted to be meeting with more children every day, yet I was finding it hard to find a stopping point. When I find myself falling into a pattern of dissatisfaction with the amount of time each group is spending together, I remind myself of what my math coach, Mimi Granados, often says to me when I ask her questions (to which she always responds with more questions!): "What is your purpose, Kassia? What is it that you want these kids to get out of this time together?"

Figure 2.2 Third-grade teacher Phoebe Markle works with a small group in a math exchange.

Returning to the issue of purpose helps me find the comfortable amount of time to work with each group. A much-repeated idea of Lucy Calkins is "teach the writer, not the writing" (1994, 228). I believe the same is true of how teaching should occur within math exchanges. I often have to remind myself to teach the mathematician, not the math. Within our brief time together in a math exchange, my purpose is not for everyone to arrive quickly and neatly at the "correct" solution. I have to practice resisting the temptation to ask leading questions or to give too much information in an effort to "fix" the errors that come out of the math exchange. This is not my job. My job is to provide many problem-solving situations that are appropriate for the children I work with and to facilitate and guide children as they bump up against challenges, questions, and new ideas.

The more you and your students practice math exchanges, the more you'll find a comfortable pace—a balance between efficiency and depth. There are always many exceptions to any rule of time—a breakthrough in thinking that leads to a longer conversation, an unplanned, spur-of-the-moment two-minute conference with a struggling mathematician. However, knowing that my purpose is not to "fix" the math but to fully use every moment together to guide mathematicians toward greater understanding helps me set my pace.

Math Exchanges over Time

More important than the exact amount of time each exchange lasts is the frequency and consistency with which you meet with students. In order to get the most power out of math exchanges, it is critical for them to be an integral part of the math workshop. Students should come to expect math exchanges on a regular basis. There are some days, some workshops, in which you may decide that your time is better spent observing students, asking probing questions to pairs of students who are playing a math game, or holding longer group discussions. Nevertheless, in any given week, math exchanges should occur three to four days per week.

Within my sixty- to seventy-five minute math workshop (in which about half my time is spent working with small groups) I usually work with two to three groups of four or five students per day. This is a group size with which I feel we can really dive deeply into the math and in which all members are active. There are enough children for there to be a diversity of ideas and background knowledge. I can facilitate a conversation in which students are talking, listening, and responding in meaningful ways. However, you have to find the optimal group size with which you can do these things. I've seen teachers work effectively with anywhere from two to six children at a time.

In deciding how frequently to meet with each child within math exchanges, I have come to believe that the answer lies in equity more than equality. Although I use a calendar to keep track of which children I have worked with most recently, I do not have a set rotation for math exchanges. There are students with whom I work more often than others. They are the struggling students (either in terms of the development of mathematical ideas, the ability to express strategies, or a lack of engagement in other parts of the math workshop). Pat Johnson, in writing about working with struggling readers, reflects upon Marie Clay's idea that "we [teachers] cannot put the reading process into the head of the child; the child must be the one to assemble the working systems" (2006, 4). Again, I believe the same can be said about mathematicians, especially those who struggle the most. As much as we may want to, teachers cannot fill a child's brain with number sense and a solid understanding of math concepts. The child must develop and construct these understandings over time with the *guidance* of the teacher and peers.

Struggling mathematicians need the most time in small groups, working not only with other struggling mathematicians but also with mathematicians who will explain in kid language why they have chosen a particular efficient strategy or what they are doing at the point of difficulty. Mathematicians need many, many opportunities to run into challenging mathematical situations that allow them to build a system of deep understanding.

As a teacher, it has taken me time to work to a place of comfort with math exchanges. I started out having math exchanges with two students and working with only one group per day. Even now at the beginning of the year I may spend so much time focusing on setting up the expectations of a math workshop that I only work with one group per day through October. I've learned to be okay with this. I have learned from experience and practice to trust in teaching deeply within math exchanges. Students are still learning throughout all the parts of the math workshop. It is okay to start small. Give yourself the time to explore how you will best facilitate these math exchanges. When I feel the "I'm-not-getting-to-work-with-enough-children" panic consuming me, I focus on this quote from Jon Muth's *The Three Questions* (2002):

> *Remember then that there is only one important time, and that time is now. The most important one is always the one you are with. And the most important thing is to do good for the one who is standing by your*

side. For these, my dear boy, are the answers to what is most important in this world. This is why we are here.

Joy, Rigor, and Empowerment Through Math Exchanges

Math exchanges involve a struggle and a grasping for deep understanding. Ellin Keene writes about teaching children "to savor the struggle." In reflecting upon struggle, Keene writes about author Reynolds Price, who through his writing "reveals his surprise at not only surviving, but thriving intellectually, and not in spite of, but *because* of his struggle" (2008, 101). Finding joy and empowerment within the rigor and struggle is a critical component and purpose of math exchanges.

Fosnot and Dolk (2001) write about the difference between "mathematics," ideas and procedures created in the past by others, and "mathematizing," constructing one's own ideas and understanding of math. About "mathematizing," they write that "when we define mathematics in this way, and teach accordingly, children will rise to the challenge. They will grapple with mathematical ideas. They will develop and refine strategies as they search for elegance; they will create mathematical models as they attempt to understand and represent their world" (13).

Math exchanges are places where children should learn to "savor the struggle" and "grapple with mathematical ideas." I know many people may be rolling their eyes at the thought of combining math, struggle, and joy. I was one of those people at one time! I understood the connection between rigor and joy in literacy teaching and learning, but math remained disconnected from this idea for me. Only when I stopped seeing mathematics as something separate from my life and the lives of my students, a system imposed on us by others, was I able to find myself as a mathematician, and, in turn, help the young mathematicians I work with view mathematics as one way of understanding our world.

3

Planning
with Purpose

Without leaps of imagination, or dreaming, we lose the excitement
of possibilities. Dreaming, after all, is a form of planning.

—Gloria Steinem

WHENEVER I AM MAKING CHANGES to the way I teach something, I want to
know what these changes will look like, sound like, and feel like for me in my
classroom. Change is hard for many of us. It is easy to continue each school
year doing things the way we did them the year before, but if we want to grow
by continually reflecting on and improving our teaching, change is inevitable.
In this chapter you will get a glimpse of several teachers as they purposefully
plan for math exchanges that spring from ongoing authentic assessment. My
hope is that you'll find pieces here that fit your own personal style and that
you, too, will be able to envision and plan for the change you want for your
own math workshop.

I am someone who likes to get to school early when the classroom is quiet
and I am (usually!) feeling fresh and recharged from the previous day. I
unlock my classroom door and walk over to my favorite round table—the one

right next to the window—where I have an amazing view of the lush green courtyard space within our school, and where goldfinches and cardinals visit the bird feeders hanging outside our classroom window. It is here, in this peaceful place I have created for myself and my students, that I start thinking about what the day's math exchanges will hold.

"Wait!" you may be saying to yourself. "You're trying to tell me you're just now thinking about these math exchanges—a few hours before you will hold them?" My answer is yes . . . and no. I am not a last-minute planner. I have already thought ahead about my focus and the mathematical ideas we will be exploring throughout various weeks. I have planned the whole-group focus lessons I will teach throughout the current week. I have used the resources available to me to design meaningful independent tasks or centers that will engage my students while I am focused on small-group math exchanges. Many times I have already written a couple of story problems I may use throughout the week within various math exchanges, based on the needs I am seeing throughout my class. But yes, it is in the morning when I sit down at my round table that I do some important thinking and planning for that day's math exchanges. I crack open the green notebook I use for planning my math exchanges. I look over my notes from the previous few days' math exchanges. What important ideas came out of those math exchanges? Should I return to those ideas today, either with the whole group or in another math exchange? Longer-term planning is critical, but a brief reflection on the previous days' math exchanges is often the most valuable planning time for me.

I decide whom I will work with that day, what our focus will be, and whether the story problems I have written earlier in the week will fit the needs of these specific young mathematicians. On a sticky note, I jot down names of students and carefully choose the numbers we will work with during our problem-solving tasks. Sometimes I write a specific question that I want to pose to the group of mathematicians as they solve the problem. Other times I want to listen to them first before crafting my words. I am imagining the possibilities of the day, and, despite the early hour, I feel the anticipation of a joyful, rigorous exchange creeping in and taking hold of my thoughts. I am ready. I can't wait to hear what they will say.

My purpose in sharing my morning routine is not to promote this kind of preparation as the only, or even the best, way of planning for math exchanges. I find joy in my early morning planning routine, but you will find the time, space, and place that feels right to you. Debbie Miller writes about being *intentional* both in your teaching and planning: "We envisioned what we wanted . . . and set about making our vision a reality" (2008, 80). Just as I have encouraged you to establish beliefs about the teaching of math, I encourage you to define your own practices and routines for planning your math exchanges.

For a long time I believed that the way in which I designed my math workshop and the way in which I worked with small groups of mathematicians should exactly mirror that of teachers whom I most admired. I am extremely lucky to work with many amazing math teachers at my school and have had the unique opportunity to teach with, observe, and talk extensively with these teachers about their beliefs and how they put them into practice in the classroom. In many cases, we share the same core beliefs about teaching and learning mathematics, so I thought that I, too, would succeed if only I learned exactly what they were doing in their classrooms and did exactly that. Wrong! I have finally learned that the way in which I translate my beliefs into practice may look different than the way someone else does it. Within the idea that math exchanges should be rigorous, but not rigid, I have found much-needed freedom as a teacher.

The Planning-Teaching-Reflecting Cycle

Regie Routman writes that "effective teaching is seamless—a good teacher moves fluidly between teaching and assessing, explanation and response, demonstration and practice, everything happening in one uninterrupted motion" (2008, 71). Planning, teaching, and assessing are all part of an ongoing cycle. It is hard to isolate one part of the cycle without addressing the others. If our goal is to teach responsively, then our planning and assessing must also be responsive to the needs of our community of learners.

I like to imagine the cycle of math exchanges as something like what is presented in Figure 3.1. Just like many aspects of teaching, the way one plans may vary greatly, even among teachers following the planning-teaching-reflecting cycle, but the basic tenets remain the same.

Many schools, including my own, use common, grade-level, multiple-choice assessments to measure students' understanding at the beginning and end of each unit. At my school we devote significant time to meeting as a team to discuss these assessments, focusing on the strengths and weaknesses we see across the grade, within our individual classes, and within the understanding of a particular child. I use this time to look at information for my class as a whole. I ask myself, "What are some common areas in which students need more instruction or time to understand ideas?"

Figure 3.1 The Planning-Teaching-Reflecting Cycle for Math Exchanges

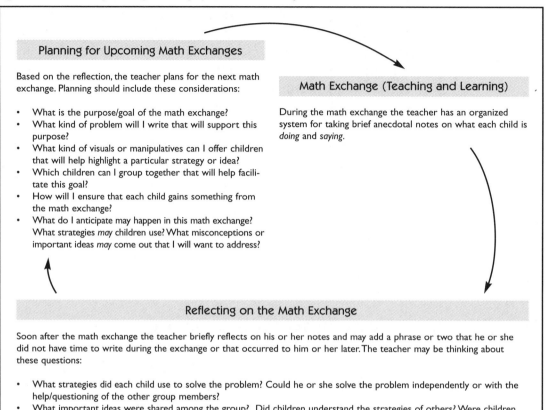

Planning for Upcoming Math Exchanges

Based on the reflection, the teacher plans for the next math exchange. Planning should include these considerations:

- What is the purpose/goal of the math exchange?
- What kind of problem will I write that will support this purpose?
- What kind of visuals or manipulatives can I offer children that will help highlight a particular strategy or idea?
- Which children can I group together that will help facilitate this goal?
- How will I ensure that each child gains something from the math exchange?
- What do I anticipate may happen in this math exchange? What strategies *may* children use? What misconceptions or important ideas *may* come out that I will want to address?

Math Exchange (Teaching and Learning)

During the math exchange the teacher has an organized system for taking brief anecdotal notes on what each child is *doing* and *saying*.

Reflecting on the Math Exchange

Soon after the math exchange the teacher briefly reflects on his or her notes and may add a phrase or two that he or she did not have time to write during the exchange or that occurred to him or her later. The teacher may be thinking about these questions:

- What strategies did each child use to solve the problem? Could he or she solve the problem independently or with the help/questioning of the other group members?
- What important ideas were shared among the group? Did children understand the strategies of others? Were children moved toward deeper mathematical understandings or more efficient strategies?
- What misconceptions or important mathematical ideas came out of the math exchange, and what conversation was had about them?
- When I meet with these children again (either together in a group or within other groups), what will be my next focus for their learning?
- How do I (the teacher) feel the math exchange went? Did I feel comfortable? Did the kids? Who did the talking? Was there an exchange of ideas? (Don't worry if you don't always think a math exchange was phenomenal. By reflecting on your own sense of how the math exchange went you'll see yourself and the math exchanges changing with more practice.)

However, most of my planning for math exchanges does not come from these common grade-level assessments, but rather from the information I gather in previous math exchanges with the children. Unlike most common grade-level assessments, math exchanges offer teachers a view of what children *can* do and *do* understand as well as what ideas are just beginning to develop in their minds. In my experience, it is this kind of ongoing, day-to-day assessment that proves the most useful for guiding our work in math exchanges.

Organizing Responsive Planning

Let's take a look at some of the common threads as well as the individual decisions of several teachers, including me, who use math exchanges as a foundational component of their math workshops.

Lauren, Kindergarten Teacher

Routines: 5 minutes
Focus Lesson: 10–15 minutes
Centers and Math Exchanges: 35 minutes
Reflection: 5 minutes

Lauren Nye is purposeful and responsive in the way that she interacts with and teaches her kindergartners—and her planning methods reflect this. Walk into her math workshop and the room buzzes with a rigorous, yet peaceful, mathematical investigation and conversation.

Planning for Math Workshop

Simplicity and purposefulness are two keys to the success of Lauren's kindergarten math workshop. Lauren creates center groups of learners with a wide range of mathematical ideas and skills who she believes will also work together cooperatively. Though Lauren's five centers remain predictable in their structure, they still allow opportunities for ample mathematical exploration, practice, and dialogue among students.

- *Exploration center:* Lauren selects exploration materials for the week from a variety of building blocks, geometric pattern blocks, dominoes, puzzles, and collections of buttons, rocks, and shells to be sorted and counted.
- *Number work center:* The content of this center varies through the year, but includes number-writing practice on a blank hundreds chart, playing numeral identification bingo, sorting numeral cards into the correct sequence, and working on hundreds chart puzzles.
- *Guided investigation:* Lauren's instructional assistant guides a task or teaches a new game from the curriculum resources available.
- *Game center:* Partners practice games previously learned and practiced with the class.
- *Computer center:* Individuals or partners play math games previously learned and practiced with the class.

Figure 3.2 Lauren's Math Centers Board

Lauren's kindergartners rotate through two centers every day, spending about fifteen minutes in each center. Students know what centers they should work in by looking at Lauren's centers board (Figure 3.2). Because Lauren herself is not part of the center rotation, she has the freedom to call students from various center groups to come work together in math exchanges. This allows Lauren to vary the frequency and length of time she meets with each group and vary which children will work in each group.

By keeping the structure of her math workshop simple and predictable, Lauren has been able to create a math workshop in which the center tasks are purposeful and at an independent level, so she is able focus on the planning and teaching of math exchanges.

Lauren's Kindergarten Math Exchanges

As Lauren's students work and play in their math centers, Lauren facilitates math exchanges. Take a look her weekly schedule of math exchanges (Figure 3.3). You'll notice that Lauren facilitates two different kinds of math exchanges—story problems and number work. Both kinds of math exchanges help kids make sense of math through conversations with peers and the teacher.

During story problem math exchanges, Lauren focuses on developing students' intuitive mathematical strategies to become effective and efficient, while also helping students understand and interpret the structure of a variety of types of story problem. When I asked Lauren how she chooses problem types and numbers for problem-solving math exchanges, she told me that she tries to focus on figuring out where the work is for the children—in the structure of the problem or in the computation of the numbers given

Figure 3.3 Lauren's Math Exchange Schedule

Math Exchange Groups				
Monday	Tuesday	Wednesday	Thursday	Friday
Penelope Seifelden Zeke (NW)	Gerson Juana Martina (NW)	Jackie Jose Brandon (NW)	Gerson Juana Martina (NW)	Jackie Jose Brandon (NW)
Sam Emilia Pablo (NW)	Ali Abdalla Christopher Nicole (NW)	Emilia Gerson Meydi Sergio (SP)	Penelope Angel Brandon Ali (SP)	Zeke Nicole Christopher Martina (SP)
Jackie Jose Brandon (NW)	Angel Meydi Sergio (NW)	Sam Seifelden Jose (SP)	Pablo Jackie Juana Abdalla (SP)	
NW: Number Work Math Exchanges			SP: Story Problem Math Exchanges	

in the problem. Once she set her goals for where she wants the challenge to be for the child, she can plan accordingly.

During number work math exchanges, children in Lauren's class work on counting and numerical patterning. These cooperative tasks help them develop and deepen an understanding of how our system of number works.

Lauren's planning and assessing notes allow her to quickly see the focus of the math exchanges on one side of the paper and use the other side to take notes on each child (see Figure 3.4). Lauren uses her notes from one week to write her math exchange plans for the following week. For blank copies of the Math Exchange Note-Taking Sheet that Lauren uses, see Appendix A.

You'll notice from Lauren's math exchange schedule and her planning and assessing notes that each child in her class participates in groups made up of different students throughout the week. Lauren forms her story problem groups by including students with a diverse range of strengths. As she puts it, "One child's strength might be in understanding and interpreting different types of story problems, but she may struggle with computation. Another child might be strong with computation, but unsure how to interpret the structure of a story problem. And there are yet other children who are great at talking about, interpreting, and comparing strategies of different group

Math Exchange Note-Taking Sheet

Week of __March 15__

Group:	Penelope, Seifelden, Zeke

Focus/Plan
Lucky the Leprechaun has _____ pieces of gold. He lost _____ pieces. How many does he have now? (12, 7)
Lucky the Leprechaun has _____ shamrocks to share between _____ friends. How many shamrocks should he give each friend so that they all get the same number of shamrocks? (9, 3)

Group:	Emilia, Gerson, Meydi, Sergio

Focus/Plan
Same problems as above.
1) 10, 5   2) 6, 2

Group:	Nicole, Christopher, Martina

Focus/Plan
Same problems as above.
1) 12, 7   2) 9, 3

Group:	Pablo, Jackie, Juana, Abdalla

Focus/Plan
Same problems as above.
1) 25, 9   2) 15, 5

Group:	Sam, Jose

Focus/Plan
Same problems as above
1) 10, 5   2) 6, 2

Group:	

Focus/Plan

Figure 3.4 Lauren developed this sheet to plan for and make notes during math exchanges for the week (page 1).

Notes on Work of Individual Children		
Penelope 3/17 1. Drew 12, crossed off 7. 2. Drew full pic of shamrock, arrows to show how many each got.	Seifelden 3/17 1. Cubes. Got 12, took away 7, "Five left." 2. Dealt 9 cubes out to 3 groups. "Three."	Zeke 3/17 1. Very similar to Seifelden. 2. " "
Emilia 3/17 1. Cubes. Got out 10, broke off 5. 2. Guessed 2 in each of 2 groups and then dealt out extras.	Gerson 3/17 1. Copied Sergio. Worked on retelling problems.	Meydi 3/17 1. Put together 10 and 5. Difficulty retelling action. 2. Unsure what to do after getting out 6. Modeled correctly after talking to group.
Sergio 3/17 1. Drew complete story. Solved by crossing off. 2. Unsure what to do after getting out 6. Modeled correctly after talking to group.	Nicole 3/19 1. Counted back. 2. Drew shamrocks and people, drew arrows to show who got what.	Christopher 3/19 1. Counted up from 7 to 12. 2. Used cubes to model, dealing out by 1s.
Martina 3/19 1. Modeled with cubes. Miscounted and took away 8 cubes instead of 7. 2. Used cubes to model, dealing out by 1s.	Pablo 3/18 1. Counted back 9. 2. Counted by 5s to solve.	Jackie 3/18 1. Started modeling w/ cubes. Changed to counting back when noticed Pablo doing this. 2. Drew picture to solve this. I helped her to apply skip-counting to see efficiency.
Juana 3/18 1. Counted back 9. Wrote number sentence "25 − 9 = 16." 2. Counted by 5s to solve.	Abdalla 3/18 1. Knew 25 − 10 = 15. "Then I put 1 back, so it's 16." 2. Counted by 5s to solve. Next time try a problem w/ skip-counting by 2s.	Sam 3/19 1. Used fingers to solve correctly. 2. Drew picture to model. Worked on retell a lot before he could solve.
Jose 3/19 1. Used cubes. Compared strategy to Sam's. 2. Could retell problem and solve w/ cubes.		
	Notes: Do backward counting by 1s (from different starting numbers) as whole-group routine next. Ask kids who seem ready if Separate Result Unknown problems could be solved by counting instead of modeling.	

Figure 3.4 Lauren developed this sheet to plan for and make notes during math exchanges for the week (page 2).

members. I want to have these children meet in math exchanges and learn from each other's strengths while also focusing on taking on the part that is challenging for them." In other words, Lauren forms groups for story problem math exchanges by a number of criteria, but heterogeneously by ability.

Lauren forms number work math exchanges by grouping children who are working on counting, patterning, and structuring numbers at the same or similar levels. She forms these groups homogenously by ability. It is important to note that Lauren's groups and schedule do not remain static. She changes who is in each group as well as how often they meet throughout the year in order to best serve her students.

Christy, First-Grade Teacher

Christy Hermann creates a true sense of inquiry and investigation in her first-grade classroom. If you pass by her classroom on any given day you will see her students creating, building, questioning, and exploring their world through mathematics. It is not unusual for her young mathematicians to grab a visitor by the hand and pull him or her into their latest investigation.

Planning for Math Workshop

Christy, whose math workshop we read about in Chapter 1, begins her weekly math planning by considering how she will manage what she calls "Explore Time," the time in which children are working in centers and coming to her for math exchanges. To organize her math workshop and make sure students are meaningfully engaged while she is working with math exchanges, Christy creates groups of two or three students who work on tasks at various centers. Take a look at the photo of Christy's Explore Time board in Figure 3.5. While it might seem overwhelming to plan enough centers so that there are only a few students working in each, Christy keeps many of her centers the same over time, changing content and adding complexity to them throughout the year.

Christy maintains five regular centers: computer, math tools, games, science project, and Ms. Hermann. Some of the centers are duplicated on any given day, so, for example, there might be two different computer centers. This gives Christy the flexibility to spread centers out across the room to fully utilize the space and lessen the noise in any given area. Every week or so she changes the tasks at the math tools stations. During the week shown in Figure 3.5 there are two math tools centers: (1) a center in which children sort coins to create combinations of a certain quantity of money and (2) a center that is

Figure 3.5 Christy's Explore Time Board

a store in which children buy and sell plastic food by finding the appropriate combination of coins to do so. Every few weeks Christy teaches the children a couple of new computer games that they can choose from when they are at the computer center. Similarly, at the games center children choose from a selection of math games that they have played many times before. These are games that they can play at an independent level with a partner without the help of the teacher. Christy also integrates a science task within her centers to review a concept they have been learning during science workshop. Christy facilitates her math exchanges in the Ms. Hermann center, where she meets with each small group of students twice weekly.

To give students a sense of a common purpose, Christy's math workshop revolves around mathematician statements, many of which you have read about throughout this book. During her class reflection time at the end of math workshop, Christy gathers students to ask them how they utilized their particular centers to practice the mathematician statement the class has been focusing on.

Unlike Lauren's math workshop, Christy is part of the center rotation, which means she meets with each group of children at least once per week. Earlier in the school year Christy's centers lasted fifteen minutes, and children would rotate to two centers every day. Later in the school year Christy found that her students benefitted from and enjoyed longer periods of time at one center. She changed her math workshop so that students worked in one center per day for thirty minutes. By remaining flexible in the structure of her math

Math Exchange Note-Taking Sheet

Week of ____February 14_____

| Group: | Juan, Jaley, Ana |

Focus/Plan
Juan has 10 cookies to share between his 2 friends Jaley and Ana. How many cookies will each friend get?

| Group: | Jorge, Eva, Soledad, Rhana |

Focus/Plan
Same problem as above.

| Group: | Jair, Melanie, Aaron, Zaida |

Focus/Plan
Same problem as above with 12 and 3 as numbers.

| Group: | Jocelyn, Preston, Nafeesa |

Focus/Plan
Same problem as above with 3 and 2 as numbers. (Getting into fractional pieces.)

| Group: | Andrew, Cristian, Carolina, Abigail |

Focus/Plan
Same problem as above with 16 and 4 as numbers.

| Group: |

Focus/Plan

Figure 3.6 Christy's Math Exchange Notes (Page 1)

Notes on Work of Individual Children		
Juan Said there could be 5 and 5. "That would be fair because 5 + 5 is 10." Ready for harder numbers.	Jaley Counted out 10 cubes. Passed them out 1 by 1 between 2 piles. Difficulty making connection to Juan's idea.	Ana Drew 2 people and 10 cookies. Drew lines between cookies and people.
Jorge Trial and error. LOTS of recounting!	Eva Started by adding 10 + 2. Then Ana helped her retell story. She used Ana's strategy. Does she really understand problem?	Soledad Modeled with cubes. But then said, "Oh, yeah, because 5 + 5 = 10."
Rhana Solved with 5 + 5 = 10. I said, "What if it was 12 cookies?" He said 6 because "6 + 6 = 12." Ready to move on to harder numbers.	Jair Modeled w/ cubes. Gave 3 to each friend, then went back to pass out extras.	Melanie Knew "4" mentally, but couldn't explain how she knew. Is she skip-counting mentally? Work on strategy explanation.
Aaron Got out 12 cubes, took away 3. Said, "Nine." Worked with him on listening to others retell and then retelling himself.	Zaida "Everyone gets 3 because 3 + 3 + 3 . . . No, everyone gets 4 because 4 + 4 is 8 and 4 more is 12." Combination of skip-counting and counting on. Used number sentence to explain ideas.	Jocelyn Drew picture of each friend w/ 1 cookie. Then halved second cookie. Taught her notation for $\frac{1}{2}$.
Preston Unsure what to do with extra cookie. "You could give it to the teacher."	Nafeesa Drew picture of each friend w/ 1 cookie. Then halved second cookie. Taught her notation for $\frac{1}{2}$.	Andrew Modeled dealing 16 out to 4 piles by 1s.
Cristian Predicted 4 and then confirmed by modeling.	Abigail Got out too many, then too few. Try again w/ 10 and 2.	Carolina Modeled w/ drawing.
	Notes: Next week get into sharing that results in fractional pieces for all groups. One-half for some groups. One-fourth for groups that are ready for it.	

Figure 3.6 Christy's Math Exchange Notes (Page 2)

workshop, Christy is able to evaluate her math workshop structure periodically and make changes that work for her community of learners.

Christy's First-Grade Math Exchanges

Like Lauren, Christy forms groups for math exchanges by balancing the problem-solving and computational strengths and challenges of her students. As you'll notice from her anecdotal notes (Figure 3.6), Christy often has a common focus and story problem throughout the math exchanges she works with, varying the numbers each group uses. Christy's notes allow her to easily see both the focus and problems she has planned for the week as well as the data she collects on each student. Looking at the data collected in her notes, Christy plans for the next week, rearranging the groups and setting new goals for the following week's math exchanges.

Kassia, Third-Grade Teacher

During my first year as a math coach, I had the unique opportunity to loop up from second to third grade and continue teaching my previous year's students for part of the day while I coached my colleagues during the other part of my day. Watching this group of students grow mathematically for two years greatly impacted my teaching practice in general and in particular my work with math exchanges.

Planning for Math Workshop

Flexibility is something I value highly in planning my math exchanges. Like Lauren, I do not have math exchanges as part of a center rotation, but rather call students from where they are working in their various independent and group investigations to come work with me in a math exchange. This way I have the freedom to mix up the math exchange groups more often and see some students more frequently than others for a period of time. This approach to organizing math exchanges also allows me to have children working in many different groups of their classmates over a period of time.

Take a look at my math workshop visual organizer (Figure 3.7). I like to map out the plan and flow of the math workshop in a way that students can easily read and understand. I give kid-friendly terms to the various contexts. For example, the students come to know that "math meeting" is our time for discussing routines and having a math focus lesson. When students know how the structure of the math workshop will unfold, they feel more control

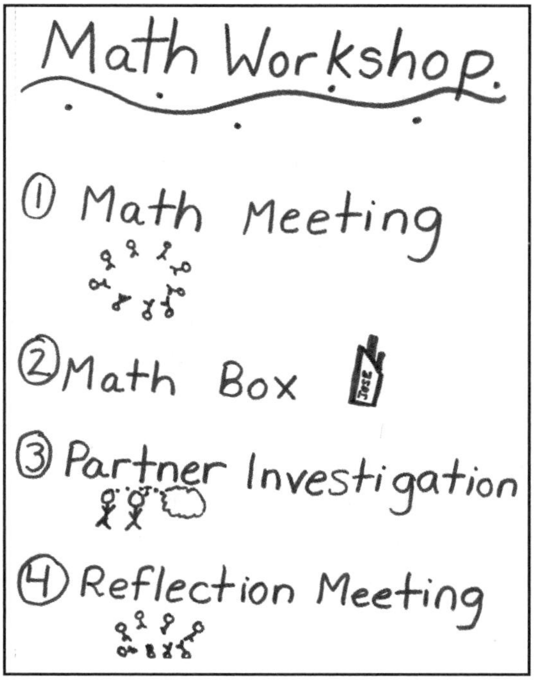

Figure 3.7
Math Workshop
Visual Organizer

and ownership over the math workshop. They concentrate better on their math thinking without worrying, "Am I in the right place?" "How long will I stay here?" and "What is going to happen next?"

After math meeting, we break out from the whole group and I begin working with math exchanges while other students begin their math box time. Similar to book boxes in many reading workshops, each student has a magazine box in which he or she keeps his or her work for math box time. In my classroom this includes a counting and patterns journal, a notebook of story problems students have completed independently and in math exchanges, and any ongoing project materials they need. As students settle into the math box time, I call my first group for a math exchange. During the quiet math box time, light music plays as the other students work independently on a task for about fifteen minutes. After this time, I ring a chime to signal that they can either continue working in their math boxes or transition to their partner or group investigations. While the content of the partner investigations is similar to what students do in centers in other classrooms, my preference is for students to work in smaller partner groups on various mathematical tasks. Most weeks I choose the partners, balancing different strengths and goals that I want to encourage in the partnership. Occasionally I will ask students to write down who they think will be a good math partner for the week, and I form groups from their suggestions.

Rather than having kids work in assigned centers, I like to give students a choice of partner investigations so they can explore what interests them most within the choices I offer. This structure is not difficult for my students to adapt to because they have been used to the center concept while in K–2 classes at our school. This structure for partner investigations is a natural extension of a center-based workshop for older students. They are familiar with working collaboratively and independently, a foundational element of all math workshops. At the end of our partner investigations and math exchange time, we gather again for a reflection meeting.

My Third-Grade Math Exchanges:
Using My Math Exchange Notebook

Being in the practice of following the planning-teaching-reflecting cycle (Figure 3.1) helps me be the best facilitator and instructional guide for my students that I can be. As I look back through my notes from the last few math exchanges, I use the cycle as a guide to question myself about both my students' progress and the instructional moves I make as the teacher.

As I've mentioned earlier, I have a special notebook that I use to organize everything I need for math exchanges. This notebook holds the notes and materials I consult on a daily basis for planning math exchanges. In it I keep the following:

1. Problem Types: Even though I have been working with the problem types discussed in Chapter 4 for years, a chart of problem types still helps me to organize my thoughts when writing story problems and planning which kind of problem I want to use in a particular math exchange. Appendix B lists and describes these problem types. You may want to make a copy of this to keep in your notebook.

2. Math Exchanges—A Month at a Glance: The month-at-a-glance organizer (Figure 3.8) allows me to quickly see with what frequency I have been working with each student in my class. For a blank copy of this organizer, see Appendix C.

3. Calendar of Math Exchanges: I use this calendar to record which groups I have worked with each day. Looking back on this calendar (see Figure 3.9), I can see not only when I met with each child but also whom each child has worked with in previous math exchange groups. This allows me to balance groups in the future and make sure each child is working with a variety of different mathematicians over time. For a blank copy of this calendar, see Appendix D.

4. A selection of problem-solving math stories: I keep both math stories I'm currently using and those I've used in past math exchanges that I might want to pull out and use again at an opportune moment.

5. All of my notes on students, recorded using the anecdotal note-taking sheet developed by kindergarten teacher Lauren Nye. (See Figure 3.4. For a blank copy, see Appendix A.)

My notebook guides my reflection on and planning for math exchanges. Let's take a look at my thoughts and notes on some recent math exchanges and at how I used a careful reflection process to plan the next steps for a

Math Exchanges—A Month at a Glance				
Month __March__				
Student's Name	Week 1 Dates: 3/1–3/5	Week 2 Dates: 3/8–3/12	Week 3 Dates: 3/15–3/19	Week 4 Dates: 3/22–3/26
Alejandra	//	///	//	/
Antonio	//	/	//	/
Blanca	///	///	///	////
Brandon	/	/	//	//
Coleman	//	/	///	//
Diana	//// /	////	///	//
Eden	//	/	/	//
Erik	///	/	/	///
Flor	////	////	///	/
Hunter	///	///	///	//
Jaime	//	///	////	///
Kyara	//	//	//	//
Lea	/	//	/	/
Maia	/	//	//	/
Marla	//	/	/	/
Miguel	//	/	//	//
Narmi	//	//	///	//
Rafa	/	//	/	/
Sandra	///	//	//	///
Yuku	//	//	//	//

Figure 3.8 Math Exchanges—A Month at a Glance

Figure 3.9 Calendar of Math Exchanges

Calendar of Math Exchanges

Note: This is an example of a calendar I used to plan four weeks of instruction. I started my next calendar with the last days of March and first days of April.

Month ___March 2010___

Monday	Tuesday	Wednesday	Thursday	Friday
1 Flor, Diana (Intervention) Alejandra, Diana, Antonio, Erik, Blanca Marla, Kyara, Yuku, Miguel	**2** Flor, Diana, Hunter, Jaime, Lea Brandon, Coleman, Eden, Maia	**3** Flor, Diana (Intervention) Alejandra, Hunter Narmi, Sandra Antonio, Erik Rafa, Blanca	**4** Flor, Diana, Marla, Sandra Coleman, Erik, Narmi, Melanie, Miguel	**5** Flor, Diana (Intervention) Eden, Hunter, Jaime, Kyara Sandra, Yuku Melanie, Blanca
8 Flor, Diana (Intervention) Alejandra, Hunter, Jaime, Yuku Antonio, Brandon, Kyara, Maia, Rafa	**9** Flor, Melanie, Blanca Diana, Narmi, Lea, Marla	**10** Flor, Diana (Intervention) Alejandra, Hunter, Jaime, Kyara Narmi, Sandra, Blanca	**11** Flor, Sandra, Melanie, Blanca Diana, Erik, Maia, Miguel	**12** Flor, Diana (Intervention) Alejandra, Jaime, Coleman, Hunter Rafa, Yuku, Lea, Eden
15 Alejandra, Coleman, Diana, Flor Hunter, Jaime, Melanie, Blanca	**16** Antonio, Brandon, Maia, Yuku, Miguel Jaime, Narmi, Sandra, Blanca	**17** Alejandra, Antonio, Coleman, Kyara, Miguel Diana, Flor, Hunter, Jaime	**18** Brandon, Eden, Erik, Maia, Rafa Narmi, Sandra, Melanie, Lea	**19** Coleman, Hunter, Kyara, Yuku, Blanca Diana, Flor, Jaime, Narmi, Marla
22 Brandon, Coleman, Eden, Rafa Erik, Jaime, Kyara, Sandra, Blanca	**23** Alejandra, Antonio, Erik, Maia, Marla Flor, Hunter, Sandra, Melanie	**24** Diana, Narmi, Sandra, Miguel Jaime, Kyara, Yuku, Blanca	**25** Brandon, Eden, Erik, Yuku Flor, Hunter, Narmi, Blanca	**26** Coleman, Diana, Sandra, Melanie, Blanca Jaime, Rafa, Miguel, Lea
29	**30**	**31**		

group of first graders. (The problem types I refer to are discussed in detail in Chapter 4.) Veronica, Enrique, Tariq, and Jose were solving Separate Result Unknown problems this example week. (Figure 3.10 shows my planning and note-taking sheet for the week, through Wednesday.) On Monday the group worked on this problem:

> This weekend Jose went to the apple orchard and picked 14 apples. He used 7 of his apples to bake a pie. How many apples does Jose have now?

When I'd composed this problem for Monday's math exchange, I'd wondered how many of these students would see the numerical relationship between $7 + 7 = 14$ and $14 - 7 = 7$. I knew that of these four children, Enrique and Jose sometimes used their knowledge of doubles facts to solve join or addition problems. However, rarely had I noticed them using facts of numerical relationships to solve separate or subtraction problems. I knew that all the children in this group would understand and at least be able to make an attempt to solve this problem through a direct modeling or counting strategy. I knew Veronica and Tariq might struggle with this problem. Both of these students had ongoing difficulty counting back from teen numbers and therefore would have to rely on directly modeling the problem with manipulatives or drawings to solve the problem. However, because we had been practicing counting backward from various numbers during the routine part of our math workshop, when I composed the apple problem I was wondering if they might try out a counting strategy rather than a direct modeling strategy.

When planning for Wednesday's math exchange, I looked at my notes from the apple problem work on Monday. I noticed that on Monday, as I expected, all students had some strategy for solving the problem. Upon seeing this, some teachers might be tempted to move on to more difficult problems. However, I knew that I needed to take a closer look at my students' strategies to see exactly what they understood and what they did not yet fully understand.

On Monday, Veronica, Enrique, and Tariq had solved the problem using a direct modeling strategy. All four students understood the language and structure of this problem, which was excellent since they are all English language learners still developing these skills. Veronica, Enrique, and Tariq were comfortable in their modeling strategies. However, their comfort with these strategies meant that they did not seem to think deeply about the numbers before jumping into this problem. They may have been ready to use more sophisticated strategies, but something about this problem did not encourage the use of these strategies.

Math Exchange Note-Taking Sheet

Week of ___9/13–9/17___

Group:	Veronica, Enrique, Tariq, Jose (Monday, 9/13)

Focus/Plan   Solve Separate Result Unknown (SRU) problems that encourage counting and fact/numerical relationship strategies.

This weekend Jose went to the apple orchard and picked 14 apples. He used 7 of his apples to bake a pie. How many apples does Jose have now?

Group:	Veronica, Enrique, Tariq, Jose (Wednesday, 9/15)

Focus/Plan   Solve Separate Result Unknown (SRU) problems that encourage counting and fact/numerical relationship strategies. Do the numbers 20 and 10 encourage different strategy use than what was used on Monday?

During art class Veronica had a box of 20 colored pencils. She gave 10 colored pencils to Tariq. How many colored pencils does Veronica have left?

Group:	Veronica, Enrique, Tariq, Jose (Friday, 9/17)

Focus/Plan   Solve Separate Result Unknown (SRU) problems that encourage counting and fact/numerical relationship strategies.

For snack Tariq brought a bag of (20/20/12) grapes. He ate (17/2/6) grapes. How many grapes are still in the bag?

Group:	

Focus/Plan

Group:	

Focus/Plan

Group:	

Focus/Plan

Figure 3.10 I used this sheet to plan a week's math exchanges for one group (page 1).

Notes on Work of Individual Children		
Veronica, 9/13 Drew 14 apples, crossed out 7, counted 7 remaining. Said, "Seven."	Enrique, 9/13 Got out ten stick and 4 ones cubes. Took 4 ones away. Covered 3 cubes from ten stick and counted 7 remaining cubes.	Tariq, 9/13 Counted out 14 Unifix cubes and placed them on hundreds chart. Took 7 cubes away. Looked at number on hundreds chart to see what number was under last cube. Said, "Seven."
Jose, 9/13 Started at 14, counted back 7 using fingers to track. Said, "Seven."		
Veronica, 9/15 Got out 20 Unifix, took 10 cubes away, counted 10 remaining. Said, "Ten." After listening to Enrique, could repeat and model his strategy.	Enrique, 9/15 Said, "It's like counting backwards by 10s. Twenty, 10. Veronica has 10 pencils."	Tariq, 9/15 Placed 20 Unifix cubes on hundreds chart. Then swept away a row of 10 cubes and said, "Ten," because "this whole row is 10 and so I didn't have to count it."
Jose, 9/15 Said, "Ten," immediately. "Because I know that 10 + 10 = 20 so 20 − 10 = 10."		
	Notes: Work on making connection of seeing and using facts/numerical relationships to solve other problem types.	

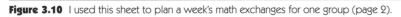

Figure 3.10 I used this sheet to plan a week's math exchanges for one group (page 2).

Jose, on the other hand, used a counting strategy to solve the problem. Following our math exchange on Monday, I noted that he was able to successfully and fluently count backward starting at fourteen and stopping at seven. However, I knew from previous math exchanges that Jose knew and could apply the doubles fact $7 + 7 = 14$ when solving addition problems, so it was still concerning to me that he did not yet do this with subtraction problems.

When I was preparing for Wednesday's math exchange I thought about Monday's math exchange to plan my next steps. How could I encourage this group to use counting and fact/numerical relationship strategies when solving separate or subtraction problems? The choice of numbers when designing story problems is key. I decided that for Wednesday's math exchange I would write another Separate Result Unknown problem for this group using the numbers 20 and 10. I was wondering if the inverse relationship between addition and subtraction would stand out more with these numbers.

I again took notes during Wednesday's math exchange using the new numbers (20 and 10) and looked at these notes to plan Friday's math exchange. From the notes and thinking about Wednesday's exchange, I realized that the new numbers helped Jose connect and apply his knowledge of the inverse relationship between addition and subtraction. Enrique connected our recent practice of counting forward and backward by tens to the problem to use a counting strategy to solve the problem. Tariq was close to being able to use Enrique's strategy. He explained Tariq's strategy in his own words during the math exchange, but still needed the Unifix cubes and the hundreds chart to solve it himself. Veronica still needed to directly model this kind of problem. Her counting was not as secure as that of the other children, so while she may be beginning to understand the strategies of the other group members, she still needed to directly model the problem to solve it independently.

I decided that we'd finish the week by solving one more Separate Result Unknown problem using the numbers 20 and 17, 20 and 2, and 12 and 6 to encourage counting on (numbers close to one another, like 20 and 17, encourage counting on), counting back (numbers far apart from one another, like 20 and 2, encourage counting back), and use of doubles facts.

As you can see, my planning and teaching of math exchanges is dependent on my continual reflection on what has happened in past math exchanges. I make a habit of asking myself, "What are my students saying, thinking, and doing?" Although I wrote my week's general plan of solving Separate Result Unknown problems with this group in advance, the details of how I wrote the problems, chose numbers, and developed the language I used to guide my math exchanges depended on my continual use of the planning-teaching-reflection cycle.

Planning for the Struggling Mathematician

Planning for struggling students is one of our greatest challenges as teachers. It is easy to become overwhelmed by what students cannot do—to focus on everything they "aren't getting" and don't know. I have learned that it is far too easy to slip into a defeatist mind-set when I focus on what a child "should-know-by-now-but-doesn't." Purposeful and effective planning does not begin by focusing on what a student does not know.

When I am uncertain about where to go next with a struggling student, it is usually a sign that I need to take a deeper look at his or her work and words in order to get a better grasp on his or her thinking and understanding. Using the "Analyzing Student Work, Thinking, and Understanding" chart focuses how I plan the next steps for this student. (See Figure 3.11 for an example and Appendix E for a blank copy of this chart.) It is helpful to utilize this chart about once every couple of weeks with struggling mathematicians.

Let's take a look at the process that my colleague Elizabeth Levine and I used for understanding third grader Evan's recent work and thinking, and how that process led us to choose where to go with our next few math exchanges with Evan. Evan is a child who has struggled for the last couple of years. I have worked with his teachers in both second and third grades and taught him directly in a before-school group. Evan struggles to remember and internalize patterns. Often it seems that he grasps something one day only to forget it the next day. He is an enthusiastic learner who wants and asks for help; however, he is beginning to realize that he struggles more than many other children, and this has an effect on his self-confidence.

Elizabeth and I met in October to talk through what she was noticing in math with Evan and to brainstorm some possible interventions and strategies. We used the "Analyzing Student Work, Thinking, and Understanding" framework developed by Bailey's math coaches Mimi Granados, Jessica Shumway, and myself. Elizabeth and I used this tool to identify what we noticed about Evan's mathematical thinking (data gained through his math interview assessments and the work he produced in math exchanges), to decide what we thought he knew and did not yet know based on this data, and to decide on next steps for his math exchanges with Elizabeth (see our notes in Figure 3.11).

Because Elizabeth and I were very specific both in laying out what Evan did and did not understand and in setting next steps for him, we were able to go back after about a month to check on his progress as a result of the

Analyzing Student Work, Thinking, and Understanding

Name and Grade: Evan, third grade _____   Date: 10/16/10 _____

Evidence of Student Thinking	What Can the Student Do?	What Can the Student Almost Do/Not Yet Do?	Next Steps
Noticing ➞	Interpreting ➞		Responding
Smooth counting through 100, after 100 will either give up or say 110.

Counts by tens to 100. Refuses to count past 100 or says, "Ten hundred," after 100.

Often skips numbers or gets stuck when counting by fives to 100.

When figuring out what number before ____ or after ____ often cannot recall numerical patterns to answer, especially with decade changes.

When solving 34 + 14, Evan uses one of the following strategies:

1) Starting at 34 on the hundreds chart, counting on 14 by ones.
2) Building 34 and 14 with tens and ones. Combining tens and ones and counting, "Ten, 20, 30, 40, 41, 42, 43, 44, 45, 46, 47, 48."

When solving 31 − 17, Evan uses one of the following strategies:

1) Starting at 31 on hundreds chart, counting back 17 by ones. | Understands and applies counting pattern by ones through 100 when starting from 1.

Can build numbers using ones cubes and tens sticks.

Has a strategy for solving two-digit and three-digit problems with sums under 100.

Understands, interprets, and solves Join Result Unknown and Separate Result Unknown problems. | Struggles to count by tens, fives, and twos.

Difficulty recalling and continuing (or perhaps doesn't fully understand) numerical patterns when counting over 100 or when counting does not begin at 1.

Only surface level understanding of decomposing numbers and seeing tens/ones relationship. Does not yet use this relationship to solve problems using efficient addition and subtraction strategies.

Struggles linguistically to understand structure of story problems when they are not the most straightforward types of problems. | At beginning of math exchanges Evan will count independently or circle-count with the group by ones and tens (and then fives and twos) starting at various numbers. We will identify patterns we notice, charting them so that we can return to these ideas.

Continued practice building numbers with base ten blocks or Unifix cubes and organizing them in the way that is easiest to count. Recognize that in the number 34 the 3 digit means 30 and 4 digit means 4.

Connect what Evan is doing with the tens sticks and ones cubes to a written representation. For example, Evan can solve 34 + 14 by adding: 30 + 10 = 40
40 + 4 = 44
44 + 4 = 48.
This is essentially what he is doing now with the blocks but he may need this pointed out. "So, what you're doing is this . . ." and then write what he is doing in form above.

When subtracting 31 − 17, after Evan takes away a ten stick and says, "Ten," ask him: "How much more do we need to take away? Where could you get that 7 from? What can you do if you need |

Figure 3.11 Analyzing Student Work, Thinking, and Understanding for a Third-Grade Student

2) Building 31 with tens and ones. Takes away one ten stick from 31 and then gets stuck not knowing where to continue taking away from. Understands structure of Join Result Unknown and Separate Result Unknown problems, but struggles to figure out what to do with Change Unknown, Start Unknown, and Compare problem types.			to take 7 from a ten stick?" This may help him at least develop this modeling strategy for subtraction with a tool he is currently using before going on to more sophisticated strategies. Continued experience with different kinds of problem types. Work on retelling problem types that are more difficult for him. More practice in risk taking while problem solving so he knows it's okay to take a chance and be wrong. **How Will I Know?** Evan will be able to count fluently to 200 by ones, twos, fives, and tens. Ones and tens will probably come first. Evan will be able to use more sophisticated strategies (decomposing numbers, tens and ones, incremental) to add and subtract two-digit numbers. Evan will expand the types of problems he understands to Join Change Unknown and Separate Change Unknown, and Multiplication.

Figure 3.11 Analyzing Student Work, Thinking, and Understanding for a Third-Grade Student *(continued)*

interventions. We found that Evan was inconsistent in his gains. Some days he was able to count to 200 (and beyond) by ones, twos, fives, and tens, and on other days he needed to be reminded of the decade numbers when counting to 50. Evan made some gains in developing more efficient strategies for problem solving that reflected a deeper understanding of how numbers work. In one math exchange with Elizabeth, Evan solved 54 + 23 mentally. Although explaining his strategy was still challenging for Evan, he solved the problem in this way:

$$50 + 20 = 70$$
$$4 + 3 = 7$$
$$70 + 7 = 77$$

However, when Elizabeth tried writing Evan's strategy on paper to help him make a connection with a written representation of his thoughts, he had difficulty understanding or applying the written notation.

Evan's mathematical challenges were not solved overnight—or in a month. He still struggles today. However, our careful reflection on Evan as a mathematician and specific interventions did lead to measurable gains. Later in his third-grade year, Elizabeth's notes on her work with Evan served as evidence of authentic, ongoing assessment and intervention that led to Evan being tested for and qualifying for special education services related to memory and processing deficits. Ultimately Elizabeth's careful consideration of Evan not only led to his improvement in mathematics but also helped him get services for underlying issues that affected him in all subject areas.

Planning is a critical part of teaching—especially for students who struggle to understand. Look carefully at your students' work and at how they work. Consider what they know and what mathematical ideas and strategies they are beginning to understand. What problems and numbers will encourage students to take the next step in their understanding? What questions will you ask them? Plan and teach as if there is not a moment to lose—and there isn't! The goal of our planning work is to get the most bang from our buck from every teaching moment.

4

Understanding Problem Types and Children's Strategies

The thesis of CGI is that children enter school with a great deal of informal or intuitive knowledge of mathematics that can serve as the basis for developing understanding of mathematics of the primary school curriculum.

—Thomas Carpenter, Elizabeth Fennema, Megan Franke, Linda Levi, and Susan Empson

LAST WINTER I SAT DOWN TO COACH EMILY, a teacher with several years of experience. She wanted to talk more about problem solving after a grade-level team meeting. During that meeting, another first-grade teacher had discussed her math workshop, in which problem solving plays a central role. "I've heard a lot of other teachers talking about different problem types, children's strategies, and how to interpret and respond to children's ideas," Emily began. "But I've got to be honest. I just don't think I'm getting it all. I'm not sure how this whole thing is a lot different than having the kids work on word problems and talk about them. I know there must be more to it and I'm just not sure where to begin."

An Introduction to Cognitively Guided Instruction

Emily was referring to a conversation between a group of first-grade teachers experienced with the work of Carpenter et al. regarding Cognitively Guided Instruction (CGI). As a teacher, I have been greatly influenced by Thomas Carpenter, Elizabeth Fennema, and their many colleagues who, through decades of research and study of children's problem-solving strategies, have changed and challenged how many people view mathematics instruction.

As my colleague Emily was talking, however, I was reminded of when my own math coach introduced me to the problem types and basic ideas behind CGI. Like Emily, I remember thinking, "What's the big deal?" as I looked over the problem types defined by Carpenter and Fennema. "How is this going to change how I teach math?"

Luckily, with the help of my math coaches and groups of colleagues, I continued to study and practice CGI and learned that CGI is much more than understanding problem types. CGI maintains the philosophy that children are problem solvers who enter school with intuitive strategies. We, as teachers, can build upon students' intuitive ideas as we guide them to deeper mathematical understanding. In the introduction to *Children's Mathematics: Cognitively Guided Instruction* (1999), Carpenter et al. write that "if we want to give children the opportunity to build their understanding from within, we need to understand how children think about mathematics. This book is about understanding how children's mathematical thinking develops and reflecting on how to help children build up their concepts from within" (xiv).

In this chapter, I provide an overview of the CGI problem types to help make them relevant to your work with your students. You may want to make a copy of the chart in Appendix B to keep in your math exchange planning notebook to help you remember the problem types and provide support as you decide on and write different kinds of problems for your students. Please note that Carpenter et al. (1999) often use abbreviations for the problem types (for example, Separate Result Unknown is referred to as SRU). For ease of reading in this book, I always spell out the problem type name. However, the abbreviations are often listed along with the full name in the figures and appendixes in this book. In addition, I discuss a continuum of strategies you might see children using to solve these problems.

Join and Separate Problems

Join and separate problems (see Figure 4.1) both involve an action—a change over time: birds fly away, children collect shells along the beach, friends eat cookies, cars navigate miles to visit grandparents. Join and separate problems are natural starting points for problem solving because they can be solved through direct modeling, a beginning strategy for most young (or older, inexperienced) problem solvers. For both join and separate problems, "result unknown" are the easiest to solve. However, even very young mathematicians can access the more difficult "change unknown" and "start unknown" problems.

Carpenter et al. (1999) describe three overarching types of strategies used by problem solvers: (1) modeling strategies, (2) counting strategies, and (3) facts and derived facts strategies. These three strategies are listed in order from least sophisticated to most sophisticated. However, as you have probably seen in your own classroom, a child using one kind of strategy with a certain problem type or certain numbers may use a very different strategy when the type of problem or numbers are changed.

Figure 4.1 Join and Separate Problem Types

Join Problems		
Join Result Unknown (JRU)	**Join Change Unknown (JCU)**	**Join Start Unknown (JSU)**
Eva had 5 cookies. Antonio gave her 10 more cookies. How many cookies does Eva have altogether/in all/in total/now?	Eva has 5 cookies. How many more cookies does she need to have 15 cookies?	Eva had some cookies. Antonio gave her 10 more cookies. Now she has 15 cookies. How many cookies did Eva have to start with?

Separate Problems		
Separate Result Unknown (SRU)	**Separate Change Unknown (SCU)**	**Separate Start Unknown (SSU)**
Eva had 15 cookies. She gave 5 cookies to Antonio. How many cookies does she have left/now?	Eva had 15 cookies. She gave some to Antonio. Now she has 5 cookies left. How many cookies did she give to Antonio?	Eva had some cookies. She gave 5 to Antonio. Now she has 10 cookies left. How many cookies did Eva have to start with?

Adapted from Carpenter et al. 1999.

Figure 4.2 shows a continuum of strategies for join and separate example problems. As you read through these strategies, think about how your own students solve problems and what strategies they might be ready to take on next.

Try It Out!

Math Exchanges Using Join and Separate Problems

Begin a math exchange with a Join Result Unknown or Separate Result Unknown problem with which you know the students in the group will be comfortable. Then, either in the same math exchange or the next day when the comfortable problem is still fresh in the kids' minds, introduce a different type of join or separate problem using the same context and the same numbers as the previous problem. The focus of this math exchange is to help children compare problems that on the surface level may seem similar, but in fact have a different structure.

Join Examples

From our classroom window we saw a grey squirrel burying nuts for the winter. She buried _____ nuts under the tree. Then she buried _____ more nuts next to the rock. How many nuts did the grey squirrel bury? (Join Result Unknown)

From our classroom window we saw a grey squirrel burying nuts for the winter. She buried _____ nuts under the tree. Then she buried some more nuts next to the rock. Altogether she buried _____ nuts for the winter. How many nuts did the grey squirrel bury next to the rock? (Join Change Unknown)

Separate Examples

On Pizza Friday the cafeteria made _____ slices of pizza. The kids ate _____ slices of pizza for lunch. How many slices of pizza were left over after lunch? (Separate Result Unknown)

On Pizza Friday the cafeteria made _____ slices of pizza. The kids ate a lot of the slices for lunch. After lunch there were _____ slices of pizza left over. How many slices of pizza did the kids eat for lunch? (Separate Change Unknown)

Helpful Teacher Facilitation Language

The language we use when guiding students is extremely important. Simply becoming more aware of and more deliberate about our teacher language

Figure 4.2 A Continuum of Common Strategies for Join and Separate Problems

Problem Type and Example	Modeling Strategies	Counting Strategies	Facts and Derived Facts Strategies
Join Result Unknown (JRU) Eva had 5 cookies. Antonio gave her 10 more cookies. How many cookies does Eva have altogether/in all/in total/now?	A set of 5 objects and a set of 10 objects are counted out. The sets are then combined into one group and that group is counted from 1 to find the total.	Counting on begins from 5 (the first number) and continues 10 more counts. Or, more efficiently, counting begins from 10 (the larger number) and continues 5 more counts.	Use of these facts: 5 + 10 = 15 10 + 5 = 15 If the numbers are 5 and 11, the child may use information derived from the preceding facts to know that: Five and 10 is 15, and 1 more is 16.
Join Change Unknown (JCU) Eva has 5 cookies. How many more cookies does she need to have 15 cookies?	A set of 5 objects is counted out. Objects are added to the set until 15 is reached. The objects added to the original set of 5 are counted to find the answer. To distinguish the added quantity, children may make a separate group as they are counting or use another color of object.	Counting on begins at 5 and continues to 15. The answer is found by keeping track (with fingers, objects, tally marks, or mentally) of the number of counts.	Use of the fact family: 5 + 10 = 15 10 + 5 = 15 15 − 5 = 10 15 − 10 = 5 →
Join Start Unknown (JSU) Eva had some cookies. Antonio gave her 10 more cookies. Now she has 15 cookies. How many cookies did Eva have to start with?	A "guessed set" of objects is counted out as the starting number. Ten objects are added to this set. The set is counted from 1 to determine if the total is 15. If not, the child adjusts the initial "guessed set" and repeats the strategy.	Counting on begins at a "guessed number" and continues 10 more counts. The answer ("guessed starting number") is found through trial and error when the child reaches 15 after counting.	→
Separate Result Unknown (SRU) Eva had 15 cookies. She gave 5 cookies to Antonio. How many cookies does she have left/now?	A set of 15 objects is counted out. Five objects are removed. The remaining objects in the set are counted to find the answer.	Counting back begins at 15 and continues for 5 more counts. The last number in the count is the answer.	→
Separate Change Unknown (SCU) Eva had 15 cookies. She gave some to Antonio. Now she has 5 cookies left. How many cookies did she give to Antonio?	A set of 15 objects is counted out. Objects are removed from the set until 5 remain. The removed objects are counted to find the total.	Counting back begins at 15 and continues to 5. The answer is found by keeping track (with fingers, objects, tally marks, or mentally) of the number of counts.	→
Separate Start Unknown (SSU) Eva had some cookies. She gave 5 to Antonio. Now she has 10 cookies left. How many cookies did Eva have to start with?	A "guessed set" of objects is counted out as the starting number. Five objects are removed from this set. The set is counted from 1 to determine if the total is 10. If not, the child adjusts the initial "guessed set" and repeats the strategy.	Counting back begins at a "guessed number" and continues 5 more counts. The answer ("guessed starting number") is found through trial and error when the child reaches 10 after counting.	→

Note: Carpenter et al. (1999) elaborate on what they call "invented strategies," which are often the most sophisticated strategies and which involve secure number sense and a deep understanding of problem solving. I have not listed the types of invented strategies in this chart; however, several examples appear throughout the book. For more information on invented strategies, see *Children's Mathematics: Cognitively Guided Instruction* (Carpenter et al. 1999).

(what we say, when we say it, how we say it) is one of the most powerful and reflective decisions we can make as teachers. Whenever I have the opportunity to watch my colleagues teach, I always find myself listening for and writing down phrases that they use that seem particularly effective and then thinking about how I can incorporate that language into my own practice. Take a look at some language my colleagues and I use during math exchanges and think about what you might take from this or change as you lead your own math exchanges.

Launching the Problem

Wow. You all solved that first problem pretty quickly and easily. I have another problem for you all. This problem is also about cookies, and we're going to use the same numbers, but I want to see if you notice anything different about this problem.

Before Students Solve

How is this problem the same as the first problem? How is this problem different?

What are we trying to figure out in this problem? What about in the first problem?

After Students Have Solved the Problem

How was your strategy in this problem different from your strategy in the first problem?

Part-Part-Whole Problems

As adult problem solvers we often view part-part-whole problems (see Figure 4.3) as very similar to join and separate problems. The thinking comes so naturally to us as adults that we have to slow our thinking down consciously in order to consider how a beginning mathematician who has not mastered the concept of the part-whole relationship may be thinking about these problems. Consider this problem:

On our class field trip to the farm we saw 15 ducks. Seven ducks were brown and the others were white. How many white ducks did we see? (Part-Part-Whole, with One Part Unknown problem)

Figure 4.3 Part-Part-Whole Problem Types

Part-Part-Whole Problems	
Part-Part-Whole, with the Whole Unknown (PPWWU)	Part-Part-Whole, with One Part Unknown (PPWPU)
Eva has 5 lemon cookies and 10 chocolate cookies. How many cookies does Eva have?	Eva has 15 cookies. Five are lemon and the rest/the others are chocolate. How many chocolate cookies does Eva have?

Adapted from Carpenter et al. 1999.

As experienced adult problem solvers we might quickly solve this duck problem by thinking of it as $15 - 7 = 8$ or $7 + 8 = 15$. However, let's take a look at some of the responses I have gotten from children:

Juan, kindergartner: Fifteen. Seven ducks were brown and the other fifteen are white. It's like you told me the answer in the story!

Gloria, first grader: Twenty-two. Fifteen ducks plus seven ducks is twenty-two.

Adam, third grader: This is impossible. You never told me how many white ducks. It just says "others" and that's not a number.

Juan's, Gloria's, and Adam's responses illustrate common misconceptions of students inexperienced with part-part-whole problems who have not yet grasped the big idea that the whole *is* the sum of its parts and the parts make up the whole.

Unlike join and separate problems, there is no explicit action or change over time to model in part-part-whole problems. The duck problem simply describes an unchanged landscape. No ducks fly away and no more ducks waddle over to the original group. Carpenter et al.'s (1999) research indicates that there is not a commonly used modeling or counting strategy that corresponds to part-part-whole problems. Children who use direct modeling as their primary strategy often find these problems difficult to solve because there is no explicit action in the story to represent or model with manipulatives. Although part-part-whole problems may be confusing to beginning problem solvers, I have found that after children understand the part-whole relationship, they quickly adapt join and separate strategies to part-part-whole problems (see Figure 4.4).

Figure 4.4 A Continuum of Common Strategies for Part-Part-Whole Problems

Problem Type and Example	Modeling Strategies	Counting Strategies	Facts and Derived Facts Strategies
Part-Part-Whole, Whole Unknown (PPWWU) Eva has 5 lemon cookies and 10 chocolate cookies. How many cookies does Eva have?	A set of 5 objects and a set of 10 objects are counted out. The sets are then combined into one group that is counted from 1 to find the total.	Counting on begins from 5 (the first number) and continues 10 more counts. Or, more efficiently, counting on begins from 10 (the larger number) and continues 5 more counts.	Use of these facts: 5 + 10 = 15 10 + 5 = 15 If the numbers are 5 and 11, the child may use information derived from the preceding facts to know that: Five and 10 is 15, and 1 more is 16.
Part-Part-Whole, with One Part Unknown (PPWPU) Eva has 15 cookies. Five are lemon and the rest/the others are chocolate. How many chocolate cookies does Eva have?	A set of 15 objects is counted out. Five objects are removed. The remaining objects in the set are counted to find the answer.	Counting back begins at 15 and continues for 5 more counts. The last number in the count is the answer.	Use of the fact family: 5 + 10 = 15 10 + 5 = 15 15 − 5 = 10 15 − 10 = 5

Adapted from Carpenter et al. 1999, 12, and Jung, Kloosterman, and McMullen 2007, 53.

Note: Children who have come to understand the part-whole relationship of these problems often transfer their strategies for solving Join Result Unknown and Separate Result Unknown strategies to solve part-part-whole problems.

Try It Out!

Math Exchanges Using Part-Part-Whole Problems

When introducing part-part-whole problems to children who are unfamiliar with this problem type, use a context that is easy for them to directly model—colors of crayons, pennies and quarters, red and green apples—something that is familiar and can be modeled using the real objects rather than representative counters. Later you can move on to more abstract contexts.

Compare Problems

Compare problem types (see Figure 4.5) are often the most difficult type of problem for children to solve. In part, this is because, like part-part-whole problems, there is no explicit action or change over time described in the problem. Compare problems simply describe a situation in which the problem solver must infer action in order to solve the problem. Consider this problem:

Eva and Antonio both collect Pokémon cards. Eva has 17 cards and Antonio has 30 cards. How many more cards does Antonio have than Eva? (Compare Difference Unknown)

Let's listen to Marco's strategy for thinking about the structure of this problem.

Marco: This is one of those hard problems like we did the other day.
Kassia: What makes this problem hard?
Marco: Well, I get out seventeen cubes for Eva and thirty cubes for Antonio. And then sometimes I don't know what to do next.
Kassia: So, what have you figured out that helps you with problems like these?
Marco: Well, it says, "How many *more* cards does Antonio have than Eva?" so I think about how many more cards Eva needs to get so she has the same number as Antonio, and then that's the answer.

Marco has clearly articulated the difficulty he and many students encounter with compare type problems. There is no action to model ("I don't know what to do next."). Many students will model the initial scenario of the problem—Eva has seventeen cards and Antonio has thirty. However, the rest of the problem stumps some kids. There's nothing here to tell us what to *do* with Eva's and Antonio's cards. There is no giving, trading, or buying of cards described in this problem. However, with practice and guiding questions from the teacher, many children, like Marco, model these problems by thinking about how many more cards Eva would need to have the same number as Antonio (a matching strategy). In other words, they have actually restructured the problem in their minds, inventing an action in the story, in order to solve it.

Figure 4.5 Compare Problem Types

Compare Problems		
Compare Difference Unknown (CDU)	Compare Quantity Unknown (CQU)	Compare Referent Unknown (CRU)
Eva has 15 cookies. Antonio has 5 cookies. How many more cookies does Eva have than Antonio?	Antonio has 5 cookies. Eva has 10 more cookies than Antonio. How many cookies does Eva have?	Eva has 15 cookies. She has 10 more cookies than Antonio. How many cookies does Antonio have?

Adapted from Carpenter et al. 1999.

Figure 4.6 A Continuum of Common Strategies for Compare Problems

Problem Type and Example	Modeling Strategies	Counting Strategies	Facts and Derived Facts Strategies
Compare Difference Unknown (CDU) Eva has 15 cookies. Antonio has 5 cookies. How many more cookies does Eva have than Antonio?	A set of 15 objects is counted out and placed in a line. A set of 5 is counted out and placed in a parallel line. The objects in the two lines are matched one to one. The answer is the remaining number in the longer line after one-to-one matching is no longer possible.*	Carpenter et al. (1999) found that counting strategies were not commonly used with compare problems.* Certainly you may see exceptions, especially if the child has inferred action in this problem to make it more similar to a Join Change Unknown problem.	Use of the fact family: 5 + 10 = 15 10 + 5 = 15 15 − 5 = 10 15 − 10 = 5
Compare Quantity Unknown (CQU) Antonio has 5 cookies. Eva has 10 more cookies than Antonio. How many cookies does Eva have?	A set of 5 objects is counted out. A set of 10 more objects is added to the first set. The answer is the new total of the set. ** (In this case a modeler has *inferred* action to the problem, adapting a Join Result Unknown strategy to a compare problem.)	Carpenter et al. (1999) found that counting strategies were not commonly used with compare problems.* Certainly you may see exceptions, especially if the child has inferred action in this problem to make it more similar to a Join Result Unknown problem.	Use of these facts: 5 + 10 = 15 10 + 5 = 15
Compare Referent Unknown (CRU) Eva has 15 cookies. She has 10 more cookies than Antonio. How many cookies does Antonio have?	Carpenter et al. (1999) found that a modeling strategy was not commonly used with this difficult kind of problem.* Certainly you may see exceptions, especially if the child has inferred action in this problem to make it more similar to a Separate Result Unknown problem.	Carpenter et al. (1999) found that counting strategies were not commonly used with compare problems.* Certainly you may see exceptions, especially if the child has inferred action in this problem to make it more similar to a Separate Result Unknown problem.	Use of the fact family: 5 + 10 = 15 10 + 5 = 15 15 − 5 = 10 15 − 10 = 5

* Adapted from Carpenter et al. 1999, 12.
** Adapted from Jung, Kloosterman, and McMullen 2007, 53.

Try It Out!
Math Exchanges Using Compare Problems

Are your students struggling with the question, "How many more . . . ?" which often appears in compare problems? Try scaffolding these problems using the questions, "How many does Eva need to have the same number as Antonio?" or "How many extras does Antonio have?" Figure 4.6 describes some of the strategies students use to solve compare problems.

Multiplication and Division Problems

Although multiplication and division are most often associated with older problem solvers, these types of problems are actually good starting points for young or inexperienced problem solvers because they are often easy to model (see samples in Figure 4.7). The terms *multiplication* and *division* and the symbols related to these operations need not be introduced to very young children, who, despite their lack of formal knowledge of multiplication and division, take quite naturally to these kinds of problems. Some of their strategies are described in Figure 4.8. I discuss multiplication and division math exchanges more fully when I describe kindergartner problem solvers in Chapter 6. Using multiplication and division problems to highlight concepts of place value is discussed in Chapter 7.

Figure 4.7 Multiplication and Division Problem Types

Multiplication and Division Problems		
Multiplication	Measurement Division	Partitive Division
Eva has 3 plates. She puts 5 cookies on each plate. How many cookies does Eva have?	Eva has 15 cookies. She wants to put 5 cookies on each plate. How many plates will Eva need?	Antonio has 15 cookies. He wants to put the same number of cookies on 3 plates. How many cookies can Antonio put on each plate?

Adapted from Carpenter et al. 1999.

❖❖❖

Our goal as teachers of math, and especially as facilitators of small-group math exchanges, is to help students understand problems and move from less efficient strategies to more efficient strategies. This kind of learning is not linear. One teacher wrote on this subject:

> *I now realize that I must be very patient, because the growth of young children as problem solvers is anything but steady and continuous. One of the teachers in our school has characterized this type of development as "bump, bump, jump" learning. Beginning problem solvers seem to "bump along," and then one day they "jump" to a much higher level of understanding.* (Buschman 2003, 543)

This is not to suggest that students' progress as problem solvers is random or completely out of our control as teachers, but rather to remind us that each

Figure 4.8 A Continuum of Common Strategies for Multiplication and Division Problems

Problem Type and Example	Modeling Strategies	Counting Strategies	Facts and Derived Facts Strategies
Multiplication Eva has 3 plates. She puts 5 cookies on each plate. How many cookies does Eva have?	Three groups are made with 5 objects in each group. The total number of objects is counted from 1.	Skip-counting by 5 is used 3 times.	Use of these facts: 5 × 3 = 15 3 × 5 = 15 If the numbers were 3 and 6, the child may use information derived from the preceding fact family to know that: Five times 3 is 15, so 6 times 3 is 3 more. So, 18.
Measurement Division Eva has 15 cookies. She wants to put 5 cookies on each plate. How many plates will Eva need?	A set of 15 objects is counted out. From the 15 objects, groups of 5 are counted out. The number of groups is counted to find the answer.	Skip-counting by 5 is used until the number 15 is reached. The answer is the number of skip-counts, usually tracked with fingers.	Use of the fact family: 5 × 3 = 15 3 × 5 = 15 15 ÷ 3 = 5 15 ÷ 5 = 3
Partitive Division Antonio has 15 cookies. He wants to put the same number of cookies on 3 plates. How many cookies can Antonio put on each plate?	A set of 15 objects is counted out. From the set of 15, objects are dealt out into 3 groups (usually beginning by one-by-one dealing, may develop into dealing by more than one or dealing a guessed amount of how many in each group). The number of objects in one group is counted to find the answer.	Trial and error skip-counting is used. "Four, 8, 12. No, that doesn't get to 15 cookies." "Five, 10, 15. So, 5 on each plate."	↓

* Adapted from Carpenter et al. 1999, 12, and Jung, Kloosterman, and McMullen 2007, 53.

child's learning path is slightly different, and that we must watch carefully to interpret students' thinking and plan next steps for their instruction.

Frequently Asked Questions About Problem Types

In my work as a math coach, I have found that many of the same questions come up from my colleagues as they begin to explore these problem types in math exchanges. Here are some of these frequently asked questions and my responses to them.

How do you decide what kind of problem type to start with?
Many teachers begin with Join Result Unknown and Separate Result Unknown problems because they seem to be the most straightforward types

of problems to solve. These kinds of problems offer an action that can be modeled for students who need to act out or draw the problem as it happens in the story. Multiplication and division problems are good places to start as well because they can be directly modeled by the student; however, sometimes these problems are overlooked as a good starting place in the younger grades because multiplication and division have not been formally introduced.

More important than what kind of problem to start with is that all students are given the opportunity to solve a variety of different kinds of problems. While certain kinds of problems are certainly more difficult than others, children who are given opportunities to solve many kinds of problems throughout the math workshop are able to access, understand, and solve all of the different kinds of problems.

Should I stay with a problem type for a certain amount of time, or should I switch the problem type with each math exchange?

As a math coach, I have seen successful teachers choose problem types in a number of different ways. I think two factors are most important in selecting which kinds of problems to give to students.

1. All students are exposed to all problem types throughout the year.
2. Teachers are purposeful in choosing the problem type.

Being a responsive teacher of math exchanges means choosing both the problem type and the numbers with specific purposes in mind. Sometimes the teacher may choose a type of problem he or she knows children will easily understand in order to focus the math exchange on the numbers in the story. For example, if I am trying to encourage or bring out an efficient strategy, such as using doubles facts to solve "near-doubles" problems, I may choose this Join Result Unknown problem:

Freddy the frog eats 12 flies on Monday. Freddy eats 13 more flies on Tuesday. How many flies did Freddy the frog eat altogether?

By choosing a problem whose context and action I know students will understand, I am guiding the thinking and conversation to focus on the numerical relationships rather than on understanding the problem type.

On the other hand, I may want the math exchange to focus on understanding comparative relationships, so I may choose this Compare Difference Unknown problem:

> Martin's pumpkin weighs 5 pounds. Catalina's pumpkin weighs 8 pounds. How many more pounds does Catalina's pumpkin weigh than Martin's pumpkin?

In this example, I have chosen numbers that are easy for my group to compute so that the group thinking and understanding focuses on understanding the problem itself.

After I choose the problem type, how do I select appropriate numbers?

Just as teachers must be purposeful and responsive in choosing which problem type to bring to the math exchange, they also must be purposeful and responsive in the numbers they choose for their groups. I choose numbers hoping to bring out or highlight certain problem-solving strategies.

When I plan for my math exchanges, I often write a problem and think of several sets of numbers I could give to various groups. Take a look at how I thought about appropriate numbers for groups of students in the primary grades solving this Join Start Unknown problem (Figure 4.9).

Figure 4.9 Choosing Numbers for Problems

On her walk to school, Carlita put some interesting rocks in her pocket. On her walk home, Carlita put _____ more rocks in her pocket. At the end of the day Carlita had _____ rocks in her pocket. How many rocks did she put in her pocket on the way to school? (Join Start Unknown [JSU])		
Numbers	**Reason for Number Choice**	**Teacher "Look-Fors"**
5, 7	Choosing small numbers like these helps me see if a student understands the problem type. Encourages counting-on strategy.	If the student randomly adds or subtracts numbers or cannot retell the story with understanding, focus the math exchange on understanding this kind of problem. You may want to stick with this kind of problem for several math exchanges in order to investigate JSU problems.
7, 15	Encourages students to use known facts (like doubles facts) to help them solve problems that are "close to" what they know.	Students who count on ("Carlita had 7 rocks, so 8, 9, 10, 11, 12, 13, 14, 15. That's 8 rocks from the morning.") Students who count back ("Carlita had 15 at the end of the day, so 14, 13, 12, 11, 10, 9, 8, 7. That's 8 rocks from the morning.") Students who use a doubles fact to help them ("I know 7 plus 7 is 14, so 7 plus 8 is 15.")
1, 100	Encourages a discussion as to whether counting on or counting back is the more efficient strategy.	Students who count on. Students who count back because they know counting back 1 is easier than counting on 100. Do students know what number comes before 100?
36, 56	Encourages making jumps of ten.	Students who count on or count back by ones. Students who count on or back by tens.
67, 100	Encourages making incremental jumps of ten and one.	Students who count on or back by ones. Students who count on or back by tens and ones.

Math Collaborative

Working together with your colleagues is the best way I can suggest to better understand the problem types, recognize strategies children use, and plan appropriate next steps for your students. Team meetings or teacher-formed study groups are a great way to start this kind of collaboration. At our Math Collaborative study group at Bailey's Elementary School, we meet to discuss books or articles related to teaching math, talk about what we're seeing in our students' work from math exchanges, and share ideas for teaching (see Figure 4.10). At our monthly meetings, I have the opportunity to reflect and think deeply with a group of colleagues. Time for true reflection is rare in teaching! We always have too much to do and too little time to do it. Our little Math Collaborative group has learned to make time for our own learning by setting

Figure 4.10 Colleagues Melanie Carney and Carol Velez discuss sample problems at a Math Collaborative meeting at Bailey's Elementary School.

a standing monthly date for the whole school year. Also, the snacks we bring to nibble on throughout our meetings don't hurt for motivation! If you don't have a similar discussion group at your school, think about starting a math collaborative. Even a small group of two or three people who want to get together to read an article or analyze student work together is a great start. I always find that I leave these collaboration meetings refreshed and ready to face the classroom again with new ideas.

Here are some suggestions you may want to try out during your team meetings or with a group of interested colleagues:

- Take five minutes each month at your team meeting to take an in-depth look at one story problem. Different teachers can take turns bringing the problem each month. What kind of problem is it? What kinds of strategies do you think your students would use to solve this problem? What kinds of misconceptions might come up with this problem? Each teacher can take a copy of the problem to use as is or to change to work with his or her own students during math exchanges.

- Try bringing student work from a common problem that teachers on your team have tried out. Bring copies of student work for everyone at the meeting. What do you notice about what the children are doing in their work? What strategies are they using? What do they understand or almost understand? What misconceptions do they have? What is the next step for each student? How can the teacher help the child get there? See Appendix E for a graphic organizer that helps with analyzing student work.

- Teachers often ask, "Will this problem solving help my students when they have to take standardized state tests?" Take a look at the word problems from a previous year's released test. (You can usually find these online at your state's department of education Web site.) You will probably notice that most of the word problems showing up on state standardized tests can be categorized into one of the problem types discussed in this chapter. With your colleagues, go through the test and classify each word problem by problem type. Do you notice any trends? When my colleagues and I did this we noticed that a lot of the problems were the more difficult compare problems. This led to some great discussions about how to facilitate effective math exchanges around compare problems.

5

Problem-Solving Math Exchanges

Mathematician Statements

These statements guided the work of the young mathematicians in this chapter:
- Mathematicians tell stories. They use math to learn about their world.
- Mathematicians learn from watching, listening to, talking to, and working with other mathematicians.

"ONE OF OUR JOBS AS MATHEMATICIANS is to tell the story of math," I say to a group of four second graders sitting at the round table with me during a math exchange. "Mathematicians for hundreds and hundreds of years have been telling the story of math. It's one way we figure out what is going on in our world." I pause for a moment to let that thought sink in, and then continue: "Do you remember when my mom, Jackie, showed us some pictures of her garden and asked us to figure out how many flowers she could plant?"

My mom had visited my classroom a few months earlier. Once the kids got past their initial shock that their teacher had a mother, they were fascinated by the photos my mom showed them of the house where I grew up, her six cats (Figure 5.1), and the hummingbirds that visit her flower garden (Figure 5.2). My mom's smaller-town experiences are pretty different from our life just outside Washington, D.C.! Since my mom's visit I have used her stories and photos in many of the small-group math exchanges I facilitate in

Figure 5.1
After my mom shared stories about her cats with my class, I featured her cats in some of our story problems.

my classroom. We've solved problems about the amount of food my mom's six cats eat in a week, different ways my mom could plant a new garden with an area of 24 feet, and those amazing hummingbirds that can beat their wings about fifty times per second. Telling stories about our lives inside and outside of school, and helping children do the same, is as important to our job as math teachers as it is as teachers of reading and writing.

Figure 5.2
My mom's flower garden also became a context for story problems.

Telling the Story of Math

Telling the story of math is very different than solving word problems written by an unknown textbook author for an unknown group of children. There is a world of difference between the "word problems" at the end of a textbook lesson and problem solving that is contextually relevant to your math community. Take a look at the word problems suggested in a lesson from your school's textbook. How can you keep the mathematical focus of the problem while also connecting the context to the lives of your students?

When I call a small group of children to work with me at the round table in my classroom or when I plop down next to several kids working on the rug, I don't immediately launch into the problem that I want them to solve. In a guided reading, the teacher gives a book introduction that intrigues the readers without giving away too much information. The teacher may introduce a new or difficult word or ask a question that activates the readers' background knowledge about the subject of the text. The same is true of a good introduction to a math story problem.

Math exchanges begin with dialogue—a flow of conversation, wonderings, and observations related to an authentic context. I am not looking to whip through a word problem with as many small groups as I can in one day. Yes, I want to make efficient use of my time, but I also know that problem solving begins with inquiry rather than numbers or equations hidden just under the surface of a problem irrelevant to the lives of those who solve it.

Math exchanges teach children not only to develop strong, efficient strategies and a deep understanding of different kinds of problems, but also to wonder, ask questions, and think about our world through mathematical lenses.

Let's return to the four second graders I mentioned at the start of this chapter so you can see some of the essential elements of small-group math exchanges playing out.

"Today I'm going to share a story with you about my mom's fish pond in her garden. Do you remember the fish pond from my mom's garden photo?"

"A fish pond is like our fish tank, but for outside," says Jennifer, looking at the photo.

"And it fits a lot more fish!" adds Michael.

"Probably more than 100," estimates Abril.

"I think more than 500 could fit, but then they might get all squished," says Abdalla, laughing.

I hold back in this conversation. I want them to talk to each other, not to me. What may at first seem like off-hand comments about the fish pond are actually the first steps these children are taking to understand the context of this story. In fact, the students haven't even seen the story problem they are going to solve yet. I've just reminded them of the photo of my mom's fish pond and invited mathematical discussion around this context. In this short dialogue between the second graders you can see both a clarification of the context and estimates about the number of goldfish that would fit in the fish pond. After a moment and a pause in their conversation I add, "Those are interesting thoughts. We've thought about different ways to estimate a lot of different things, but I'm not sure how you'd figure out how many fish could fit in a pond."

"Maybe we should ask your mom, Jackie," offers Jennifer.

"That would be one way. The problem we'll work on today will give us some information about the number of fish in the fish pond, but I bet you'll still have more questions even after we solve this problem," I say. I pass out papers with the problem typed on them. I added a picture of my mom's fish pond at the top of the page to help the children remember new language and connect to the story.

In kindergarten and first grade we work from mostly oral storytelling; however in second grade many students like to read the math story as well as hear it. Also, referring back to the text to understand the story problem is an important element of problem solving that students are learning at this age.

"Jackie had a fish pond with _____ goldfish," I read to them, saying "mmm" for the blank in which we will later write a number. "For her birthday I gave her some more goldfish. Now Jackie has _____ goldfish. How many goldfish did I give Jackie for her birthday?"

"Well, how many fish did you give her?" asks Abril. There is a pause in the group's conversation. I don't make a move to fill it.

"That's what we have to figure out!" responds Michael. The group is beginning to question, to visualize the context, to wonder. *This* is the beginning of a great math exchange.

The Importance of Retelling in Problem Solving

After I have read a story problem aloud a couple of times to the group without giving them the numbers in the story, I usually ask, "Can someone tell us what's going on in this story?" At first, children may be resistant to the idea of retelling a story problem that, as of yet, has no numbers. However, by retelling the math story without the numbers, the children can focus on mapping out the plot of the story in their minds without yet thinking about specific strategies for solving the problem (see Figure 5.3).

When I first started facilitating math exchanges in this way with my class, the children were uncomfortable. When I asked them to tell the story again without giving them the numbers, they were hesitant. "But we don't even know how many fish there are in the pond!" "Where are the numbers?" "Is this adding or subtracting?" They wanted all the information up front!

However, by slowing down the process of problem solving in order to focus on understanding the problem being solved, children focus on the context of the problem. Problem solving requires much more than simply manipulating numbers through some operation. Understanding and organizing the known and the unknown, creating a map in your mind of the problem, and selecting a mathematical process you might use to solve it are all integral parts of problem solving.

Many teachers have told me, "My students don't even bother to really read or understand a word problem. They just jump straight to the numbers and

Figure 5.3 Laura Wagner's third-grade students retell a story problem before solving it.

add or subtract them without really understanding." We can prevent this issue by withholding the numbers until students have a chance to digest the story.

Arthur Hyde, in *Comprehending Math: Adapting Reading Strategies to Teach Mathematics K–6* (2006), writes about the dangers of creating a philosophical separation between the teaching of reading and the teaching of math. "What is the fundamental message the kids get when told to look for the *key/cue* word? Don't read the problem. Don't imagine the situation. Ignore the context. Abandon your prior knowledge . . . You don't have to read; you don't have to think. Just grab the numbers and compute" (3).

Consider this example: Math instruction focused on key words tells us that the word *more* should tip us off that we will be adding numbers. But look at the following problems, which all include this complex word.

Carlos and Elizabeth go apple picking. Carlos puts 10 apples in their basket and then Elizabeth puts 5 *more* apples in their basket. How many apples do Carlos and Elizabeth have now? (Join Result Unknown)

Carlos and Elizabeth go apple picking. Carlos puts 10 apples in their basket and then Elizabeth puts some *more* apples in the basket. At the end of the day Carlos and Elizabeth have 15 apples in their basket. How many apples did Elizabeth pick? (Join Change Unknown)

Carlos and Elizabeth go apple picking. Carlos picks 10 apples and Elizabeth picks 5 apples. How many *more* apples did Carlos pick than Elizabeth? (Compare Difference Unknown)

All three of these problems include the word *more*. Children who have been taught to rely on key words to tell them what kind of computation is necessary and children who have developed the misconception that "*more* means *add*" through a lack of exposure to different kinds of problems will usually add the two numbers in these problems. Such computation will result in only answering the first problem correctly and reinforces the idea that the goal of problem solving is to weed out the words and get to the numbers. Just as we do in reading and writing, we want children to connect with the context, imagine, think, ask questions, and reason.

So, how can we help children see mathematical problem solving as this kind of process? Peter Johnston writes that "talk is the central tool of [a teacher's] trade" (2004, 4). The way a teacher uses his or her own talk to introduce a problem and facilitate students' conversation about that problem sets the stage and the expectation for the level of thinking that will occur throughout the math exchange.

Let's take a look at a recent math exchange I facilitated with a small group of first and second graders. Consider how retelling the story problem without the numbers can lead to better mathematical understanding and stronger, more accurate strategies when we do introduce the numbers.

Sarah and Mohammed found _____ wildflowers during recess. _____ were purple and the rest were yellow. How many yellow wildflowers did Sarah and Mohammed find?

This type of problem is classified by Carpenter et al. as Part-Part-Whole, with One Part Unknown. The whole (total number of wildflowers) and one part (number of purple wildflowers) are known, and one of the parts (number of yellow wildflowers) is unknown.

Some types of story problems have a structure that is easier to comprehend and solve, but the part-part-whole structure can be initially confusing to students who are inexperienced with it. In fact, when very young children are presented with part-part-whole problems such as "I have two green apples and one red apple. How many apples do I have?" it is common for them to be puzzled. Didn't you just tell them the answer? You have two green apples and one red apple. The ability to make and break groups has not yet been developed in many young children. However, with a little experience, children quickly develop strategies for part-part-whole problems.

"So, who can tell us what is going on with Sarah and Mohammed in this story? What do you think, Judy?" I ask a particularly quiet girl in the group. I want to give her a chance to contribute her thoughts before the rest of the group jumps in.

"Sarah and Mohammed see flowers," Judy replies in an almost inaudible voice.

"Yeah!" jumps in the never-shy Brandon. "Like those flowers that are really out there by the soccer field. Dandelions—they're the yellow ones—and then those little purple ones, I don't know their names."

"Okay, and what do we know about those flowers that Sarah and Mohammed found? Can you tell us more, Judy?" I ask.

"There are yellow and purple flowers," she replies after a long pause.

"Who can add on to what Judy has already told us?" I ask.

"We want to know how many yellow flowers 'cause the question part says, 'How many yellow wildflowers did Sarah and Mohammed find?'" says Sarah.

I pause. I can tell by the silence that a few of the kids are struggling to understand this problem. They know the problem is about two colors of wild-flowers, and we want to know how many of the flowers are yellow. However, part-part-whole type problems can be difficult for children beginning to understand groups as both a whole and the sum of its parts. There is no easy direct action to be modeled in this problem. No one is picking flowers or planting more flowers. We are simply describing a situation that exists without any obvious change or action occurring.

"So, we don't know how many yellow flowers Sarah and Mohammed found. But what *do* we know?" I prompt.

Mohammed speaks up. "We know they found 'mmm' flowers, and we know that 'mmm' of them are purple and the rest are yellow."

"And 'the rest' is like a mystery because 'the rest' isn't a number. It's just some," adds Sarah.

It sounds like Mohammed and Sarah have an understanding of the part-whole relationship, but I'm still not sure about Judy and Brandon.

"Okay, so now let's read it again with the numbers. You write in the numbers as I tell the story and then I'm going to ask you to tell the story one more time before we think about how we'll solve this problem," I say. Then I read, "'Sarah and Mohammed found thirty wildflowers during recess. Sixteen were purple and the rest were yellow. How many yellow wildflowers did Sarah and Mohammed find?' So, Brandon, can you tell the story again in your words?"

"Sarah and Mohammed found thirty flowers. Sixteen are purple and some are yellow. How many are yellow?" Brandon says.

Judy continues, "So there are sixteen purple flowers and some yellow flowers that make all the flowers add up to thirty."

Through our in-depth and repeated retellings of this story the children articulate their understanding of the part-whole relationship between purple flowers, yellow flowers, and the set of all flowers. While Sarah and Mohammed had a stronger understanding of this concept going into the problem, Judy's and Brandon's understanding strengthens as we continue to retell this story and they listen to words of their fellow group members.

This whole conversation happens within the time span of two or three minutes. The words may seem repetitive, but the idea is to guide students to a true understanding of the problem so that they choose a strategy that reflects an understanding not only of the numbers in the problem but also of the structure of the story.

Teacher Language for Story Problem Retelling

Here is some language you may want to try as you begin math exchanges in which one of your focuses is understanding the story structure through retelling:

- *Who can tell us what is happening in this story?*
- *What do we know about what is going on? What don't we know yet?*
- *What are we trying to figure out?*
- *Which number do you think will be bigger, the number of wildflowers or the number of yellow flowers? Why?* (For example, students who understand the wildflower problem will understand that the total number of wildflowers will be greater than either of the two groups of wildflowers. This question can be a good check of students' understanding of the part-part-whole structure before the group moves on to solving the problem.)

Time for Thinking

After our conversation about what the story is asking us, I give students time to work and think on their own. They may talk to someone else in the group or even spend time watching another student work, but I usually do not interrupt their thinking for several minutes. Math tools are always close by where students can reach them. I jot down notes about what students are doing, trying not to interrupt their thinking during this time with my questions. If a student truly seems at a loss about what to do, I might ask him or her to tell me the story again or ask about where he or she might begin: "Is there a strategy or a tool that might help you?" "What are you thinking about doing first?"

Even though this is a relatively independent time for thinking, I do not usually discourage children from watching each other or even mimicking what other students do or write. In the beginning of the year, children unfamiliar with math exchanges may complain, "She's copying my ideas!" or try to shield their papers from others in the group. I simply reply with one of the mathematician statements we have practiced: "Mathematicians learn from watching, listening and talking to, and working with other mathematicians."

If a child is always mimicking or copying the work of others without making an attempt to solve independently, I need to stop and think about what is going on with this child. Are the problem and numbers appropriate challenges for this student? Does he or she understand the story problem? Is this the right group for this child right now? I also consider questions to ask the child. "I notice you're thinking about Blanca's ideas. What questions do you have for Blanca about her strategy?" Is the child able to articulate a question or part of the strategy? If so, this might be a great time for a guided conversation between the two problem solvers. If not, I might proceed to some of the questions and comments that appear in the following list. Slowly but surely we build the balance of trying out our own ideas and sharing our ideas with others in order to learn from one another.

Teacher Language for Helping a Child Get Started
- *So, what are you thinking about trying/doing first?*
- *What strategies or tools have you used before that might help you with this problem?*
- *I notice Jaime using an open number line to help him keep track of and record his thinking. You've used those a lot before. Would you like to listen to Jaime's strategy to see if that gives you an idea of how to figure out this problem?*
- *Let's try changing the numbers. We'll come back to these numbers later.* (Try giving the student very simple numbers to help him or her come up with an initial way to solve the problem. In the wildflower problem you could try ten wildflowers, with eight purple and the rest yellow. Sometimes taking the numbers down to a level that is easy for the child will help the child understand the structure of the problem and then come up with a way to solve the problem when the numbers are more challenging.)

Time for Sharing and Reflecting

Sharing and reflecting on strategies used during math exchanges has a powerful impact on the development of effective and efficient strategies for problem solving. When students are working together in a small group, the focus on active listening, explaining, and responding is amplified. All group members must work together to keep the dialogue going.

Preparing Our Bodies and Space for Sharing

Whether reflecting with the whole class or in a small group, I believe sitting in a circle in which all members of the community can see one another is crucial. Since I want to encourage dialogue between the students, not between a student and myself, I start by teaching children to look out into the circle at one another (and not at only me, the teacher) when presenting their ideas. The children who are listening respond to the speaker by positioning their bodies and eyes to focus on the person speaking.

No hand raising is allowed when someone is speaking. Not only is it distracting, chances are the person raising his or her hand is focused on his or her own thoughts rather than those of the person sharing. When we share in small-group math exchanges, we learn to share without raising hands. We learn to be attentive to pauses in the conversation that signal that someone has finished a thought and that someone else can now respond. We learn to respond, agree, disagree, and add on to the ideas of others rather than abruptly change the flow of conversation to insert our own ideas. When we share with the whole class, we show a silent thumbs-up at belly button level rather than raising a hand to indicate when someone wants to share. This simply allows me to see who is ready to share while allowing others to continue thinking without being disrupting by hands waving and voices shouting, "I know! I know!"

During a small-group math exchange, I always remind children to put the caps on their pens when we are preparing to transition from independent thinking time to group dialogue. This is a simple move that signals a change from focusing on our own thinking to focusing on the group. In addition, I don't have to worry about reminding kids to stop doodling and focus on the person sharing!

As students are working during a math exchange, I think about what I want to highlight when we share strategies and ideas. Sharing and reflecting can take several different forms, several of which I describe in the following sections.

Sharing Strategies with a Focus on Different Approaches to the Same Problem

Many times in the beginning of the school year my focus for sharing is to help children recognize that there are many strategies for solving a single problem. I want them to listen to and understand others' strategies. This sounds simple, but it is a process that takes considerable time to practice, and patience. Most children—just like adults—are more focused on sharing their own ideas in a conversation than reflecting on the ideas of others.

Maria Nichols devotes her book *Comprehension Through Conversation: The Power of Purposeful Talk in the Reading Workshop* (2006) to understanding and examining the power of dialogue in the classroom. Referring to David Bohm's essay "On Dialogue" (1996), Nichols writes of the importance of distinguishing between the act of communicating and dialogue. "Communication . . . is a telling of one's ideas, making one's thinking clear to another. But dialogue . . . is coming to an intellectual exchange willing to see and hear something new in the exchange, and actually creating a newer, stronger understanding because of the exchange" (2006, 7). It is this kind of exchange we are ultimately working toward in a math exchange.

So how do we, as teachers, teach and facilitate this kind of sharing and exchange of ideas and strategies? The following are some practices I have found crucial to creating an environment of exchange in which children are as focused on understanding the ideas of others as on sharing their own experiences with the math.

Teacher Moves to Support Student Dialogue: Sharing of Strategies

Many students unfamiliar with problem-solving discussions struggle to express their strategies. They are inexperienced at explaining their thought process and some really may not have the self-awareness of knowing how they solved a problem. With some practice even very young students can become quite good at explaining their strategies. The teacher moves described in Figure 5.4 will give you some ideas of how to help students describe their strategies to others.

Teacher Moves to Support Student Dialogue: Focus on Identifying Efficiency

When I first began to teach math with a focus on problem solving, I wondered if my young students would be able to understand the concept of efficiency in problem solving. At the beginning of one year of teaching second grade, I gave some groups of students the problem $6 + 52$ to work on. I wanted to see who would use manipulatives to count three times, making groups of six and fifty-two and then pushing them together to recount from one. I wanted to see who would count on from six because it was the first number in the equation, and who would realize that counting on from the second addend, fifty-two, was not only possible, but also a lot easier and quicker.

As I worked with groups of students on this problem, I noticed a wide range of strategies. My students also noticed that while some students took a long time to solve this problem, others solved it in a matter of seconds.

Figure 5.4 Teacher Moves to Support Student Dialogue: Sharing of Strategies

Initiating Dialogue

Teacher Language	Purpose	Teacher Look-Fors and Follow-Ups
Who has a strategy for figuring out this problem?	Opening the sharing to all.	Are the same kids always volunteering to share?
Ana, I saw you working on an interesting strategy. Can you share what you have been thinking with us? Or, Ana, I think your strategy might help other people think about this problem. Will you share it when we are ready to reflect? (I usually check with this person while the students are working to make sure he or she is comfortable sharing.)	Focusing the opening of the sharing on one person. This could be a person who is sometimes reluctant to share, a person who thought about the problem in an efficient way, or a person whose strategy is similar to or different than others' strategies.	How many have a strategy they are willing to share? Are kids with more and less sophisticated strategies volunteering to share?
We are going to focus on three people's strategies today. As they share, think about how your strategy was similar to or different from those that Ana, Shereen, and Rafa used.	Sharing three strategies that are representative of others' thinking for a comparative conversation of strategies.	Which students recognize their own strategies or ideas in the work of others?
Turn and talk to the person next to you. Share your strategies. Work really hard to understand your partner's strategy by looking at his or her work and asking questions. Signal for kids to turn back into the group. (I use a shaker.) *Who is ready to share their partner's strategy?*	Giving all students an opportunity to share their strategies and practice meaningful dialogue. As a teacher, I can listen in on particular conversations to assess strategies and dialogue skills.	Who is actively listening and talking with his or her partner about his or her strategy/work? Who can understand his or her partner's strategy well enough to explain it?

Follow-Up After a Student Has Shared a Strategy

Teacher Language	Purpose	Teacher Look-Fors and Follow-Ups
Shereen shared some important ideas. Who can say how Shereen solved this problem?	Learning to restate the ideas and add on to the ideas of others.	Are children simply "parroting" Shereen's strategy word by word or are they restating a strategy in a way that demonstrates understanding?
Who can add on to what Shereen shared?	Encouraging children to listen to each other's ideas with a specific purpose in mind (rephrasing a strategy, adding on a new idea, comparing strategies).	Who can follow someone else's line of thinking and add his or her own response or idea that relates to the initial idea? Who shared an unrelated idea because he or she either lacks understanding/misunderstands Shereen's strategy or because he or she doesn't understand that his or her thought should be related to that of Shereen?
Why do you think Shereen chose to …? (Point out something important/different/efficient in the student's strategy.)	Learning to engage in dialogue that encourages thinking about their own and others' ideas.	Who understands the reason Shereen chose her strategy for this specific problem? Who simply restates Shereen's idea without addressing her reasons behind using this strategy?

(continued)

Figure 5.4 Teacher Moves to Support Student Dialogue: Sharing of Strategies *(continued)*

Teacher Language	Purpose	Teacher Look-Fors and Follow-Ups
What do you all think? Do you agree or disagree with Shereen's answer?	Demonstrating a high level of thinking by understanding and articulating someone's motivation for using a specific strategy. For example, "Shereen made the 79 into an 80 when she was adding 79 plus 14 because it's an easier number to add 14 to. Then when she got 94, she had to take out the 1 she added before to the 79. So she got 93."	Are students actively engaged in listening and evaluating the strategy for correctness and efficiency? Do children understand where someone got off track, which resulted in a wrong answer?
Did anyone solve this problem in a similar/ different way than Shereen?		Who can distinguish whether his or her strategies and ideas are similar to or different from those of Shereen? Who can articulate why they are different?
Eliciting More Information from a Student Who Has Shared an Idea		
Teacher Language	Purpose	Teacher Look-Fors and Follow-Ups
Tell us more. Or, Tell what you mean by …	Giving student opportunity to expand if his or her idea is unclear or you want to further highlight this idea.	Does the student know how to clarify ideas?
Hmm … I'm not sure I understand exactly what you mean. Sometimes kids understand each other's strategies better than adults. Does anyone understand what Rafa is telling us?	It's true! Sometimes I can be at a complete loss for what a student is saying, but other kids are nodding and connecting to the speaker's idea. Also, this reinforces to the speaker and listeners that ideas must be presented clearly and listeners must work to understand.	Is there negotiation of meaning between the original speaker and those clarifying the idea?
Keep going. You have something important to tell us.	Responding to a student stopping mid-idea or saying, "I forgot." Often a few words from the teacher will give confidence to keep going with the idea.	Do students become more confident in presenting ideas, or are they truly confused?
Can you show us how you did that?	Sometimes ideas can be hard to explain orally and are more clearly illustrated/recorded/shown by the person who thought of them.	How does the student demonstrate what he or she did? With math tools? A written strategy? A drawing?
I think it might help to see your work. Is it okay if I hold your paper up while you explain what you did?	Many times students explain their ideas from their written work, which may be hard for others to follow. Sometimes it helps if the teacher holds the work while the student shares so listeners can refer to the students' words and work.	

Figure 5.5 Teacher Moves to Support Student Dialogue: Focus on Identifying Efficiency

Teacher Language	Purpose	Teacher Look-Fors and Follow-Ups
Remember how mathematicians look for efficient strategies to solve problems? I noticed some efficient strategies when you all were solving this problem. Max, can you share your strategy with us?	Reminding children that efficiency is one of our goals in math, acknowledging that many of them were using efficient strategies, and focusing on a child whose strategy I want to highlight for efficiency.	Who recognizes that his or her strategy was similar to or different from Max's? Who can compare his or her strategy to Max's? Who can explain part or all of what Max did and why he did what he did?
Who understands some of what Max told us? Or, Eva, what part of Max's strategy do you understand?	Giving other children the opportunity to practice explaining an efficient strategy. By using the words *some of* or *part of,* I let them know it is okay not to fully understand the strategy. This is an effective way to get kids to start talking. Often they understand more than they think.	What parts of Max's strategy are highlighted? Can children identify why Max's strategy was efficient?
So, Max told us that he added six to fifty-two. Who can show us what that looks like and sounds like? Or, So, Max started counting from fifty-two. Is it okay to start with the second number in the addition number sentence?	Focusing on the specific efficient strategy (counting on from larger number). Allowing several children to practice it. "Fifty-two ... 53, 54, 55, 56, 57, 58." Focusing on a specific big idea (commutative property of addition). Students must prove why or how this works.	

Figure 5.5 shows some language I have developed over the years to use when helping children identify and use efficient strategies. It is important to remember that our goal is not always for all children to use the most efficient strategy immediately after seeing other children use it. It is unreasonable to believe that a child who is not yet counting on will fully understand and be able to utilize the strategy of counting on from fifty-two when solving 6 + 52. In fact, when a child does something like this, it is most often a product of strategy mimicking rather than full understanding of the strategy. However, it is important for children to listen to and try out different, more efficient strategies as they are ready to take them on.

When I solved 6 + 52 with a group of second graders, Eva listened to Max's counting-on strategy. "I just went 52, 53, 54, 55, 56, 57, 58," Max said, raising six fingers as he counted on. "Also, I know that 6 plus 2 equals 8, so 52 plus 6 equals 58." Eva, who had used a hundreds chart to count on fifty-two from six, listened carefully.

"What are you thinking about Max's strategy, Eva?" I asked.

"I know there's a quicker way. You can start with 52," responded Eva. Even though Eva could not fully explain Max's strategy and did not utilize a strategy similar to this one until later on in her second-grade year, she gleaned two important ideas from listening to Max share his strategy. First, Eva understood that there existed more efficient ways to solve the problem than she was using. Second, Eva began to show an understanding of the applications of the commutative property (that $a + b = b + a$). This is a huge idea! Had Eva only been working and talking with other children using her own strategy, this revealing conversation certainly would not have developed.

I know now that children can begin to understand the idea of efficient problem solving from a very young age. Some teachers I know in kindergarten and first grade use the words "quick and easy" when pointing out efficient ideas. I teach both the concept and the word *efficient* beginning at the start of first grade and teach it throughout the year, reminding children of the mathematician statement we read about earlier: "Mathematicians look for efficient ways to solve problems."

❖❖❖

Facilitating math exchanges is really an art and a science. We try to achieve a balance between carefully planned and crafted questions and conversation and more spontaneous inquiry and wonderings. Both will lead us to new ideas and the transformation of old ones.

CHAPTER 6

Kindergarten Mathematicians

Mathematician Statements

These statements guided the work of the young mathematicians in this chapter:
- Kindergartners are powerful mathematicians.
- Mathematicians explain and record their ideas in ways that other people can understand.
- Mathematicians check their work to make sure it makes sense.

KINDERGARTEN IS A POWERFUL PLACE for the learning of mathematics. For many children, this is their first experience with school and formal mathematics. For teachers, kindergarten is our first opportunity to teach these young children that math is about problem solving (see Figure 6.1). It is our first opportunity to teach children that math is not about the acquisition of rote skill; it is about acting as mathematicians to figure out the world around us. Kindergarten is our opportunity to value our students' informal life experiences with math and the intuitive strategies they bring to problem solving. It is our opportunity to provide space for purposeful math play and rich problem-solving experiences. The way we teach math in kindergarten and the way we interact with kindergarten mathematicians sets the stage for all of their future math experiences. The importance of mathematics in kindergarten cannot be overemphasized.

Figure 6.1 Kindergarten teacher Michelle Gale works with two kindergarten students during one of their first math exchanges.

Mornings are my favorite time of day in the kindergarten classroom. Children come in eager to tell stories and ask questions. Mathematics is an organic part of the day, spurred by inquiry, curiosity, and, most importantly, play. In kindergarten classes at Bailey's Elementary School many classrooms begin their day with play. It provides a smooth transition from home to school as children enter the classroom. On many days, students Yolanda and Raji begin their mornings in the play kitchen, which they have transformed into a restaurant, handing take-out menus to their friends and working the cash register.

"How much dollars is this?" Raji asks.

"Twenty dollars," responds Yolanda.

"That's too much for ice cream! Here's two dollars," says Raji, always the bargainer.

In a kindergarten class where I have been working, Henry, Amalia, and Lea are in the classroom library singing a song from one of the class's favorite children's books, *Pete the Cat: I Love My White Shoes* by Eric Litwin (2010). Inspired by Pete the Cat, they have decided to investigate all the shoes in the classroom. I have been watching this exchange out of the corner of my eye as I welcome children into the classroom and help them hang up their coats.

"I wonder how many shoes we have in our classroom," I think aloud to the group.

"A lot!" laughs Henry.

"Let's count them all," suggests Amalia. "Let me go get a clipboard and some paper."

I leave them to their investigation and walk over to a group of kids constructing a miniature model of our classroom using blocks and structures they have built from scrap paper; because we start our day with math, I bring up the shoe investigation again when the morning play time is over and we gather on the carpet to begin our math workshop. Even though I had another plan for today's math workshop, the child-led shoe inquiry seems more important to investigate today. "Henry, Amalia, and Lea are working on an interesting project this morning. They're thinking about Pete the Cat's shoes and trying to figure out how many shoes we have in our classroom."

"Yeah," interrupts Aaron. "They tried to take off my shoes!"

"We wanted to make a big pile of shoes to count," says Lea, defending the attempted theft of Aaron's shoes.

"That would be one way of figuring out how many shoes are in our class," I say. "This seems like a problem we might need the help of the class to figure out. How could we figure out how many shoes are in our class without having to take off everyone's shoes and put them all in a pile?"

With that, we have begun the work of kindergarten mathematicians. Some children pull out paper, crayons, and clipboards and start drawing stick figures wearing shoes, others start counting the number of people in the classroom, and still others start making tally marks on chart paper they have taped to the easel. We have been at school for less than an hour this morning and already we're deep into the joy and rigor of mathematics.

Kindergarten is a powerful place for the learning of mathematics. Research suggests that even children living in poverty, who enter school with significantly less mathematical knowledge and experiences, can catch up to their more privileged peers within the kindergarten year (Fuson, Clements, and Beckmann 2010, 1). Kindergartners (and indeed, prekindergartners) have been long underestimated in their ability to make sense of mathematics, problem solve, reason, and make connections. Traditional kindergarten mathematics instruction has been too narrow and skills based and has ignored the ability of kindergartners to do much more than they have traditionally been asked. This does not mean that we need to push kindergartners toward the acquisition of more individual skills. In fact, math curriculum throughout the United States has often been criticized as being "a mile wide and an inch deep" (U.S. National Research Center 1996). Greater depth of mathematical understanding should be a goal throughout the grades, but it is particularly important that we set these expectations for our youngest students.

The intuitive strategies kindergartners bring to mathematics, along with a classroom in which the teacher engages children daily in problem solving, allow these young children to solve problems that are much more complex than we traditionally have thought possible. Kindergartners come to school with so much informal mathematical knowledge, and they are ready to share it all!

What Are the Big Mathematical Ideas for Kindergartners?

The Common Core State Standards (2010) and NCTM's *Curriculum Focal Points* (2011b) are two resources I have found particularly helpful for identifying the big ideas of kindergarten mathematics. In addition, NCTM recently published *Focus in Kindergarten: Teaching with Curriculum Focal Points* (Fuson, Clements, and Beckmann 2010), which offers an in-depth look at kindergarten learners, focusing on the big conceptual ideas of math rather than isolated skills. I use these resources in addition to my own state's standards, textbooks available at my school, and the amazing kindergarten team with whom I work.

In Figure 6.2 I summarize the most important big ideas for kindergarten mathematics content within the number and operations strand. In deciding where to go next with a young mathematician, the focus should always be on what the child already knows and almost knows and how to teach from that point on. While the Common Core State Standards and the *Curriculum Focal Points* are excellent starting points for understanding kindergarten math in general, teaching should always be responsive to the needs of the individual child. I highly recommend looking at prekindergarten and first-grade standards to get a vertical view of the big mathematical ideas throughout the primary grades. In comparing these big ideas to your own state's standards, you will certainly find much overlap. My purpose in creating the table of big ideas (Figure 6.2) is to help integrate the important skills that the standards address into the broader big ideas of mathematics.

Figure 6.2 A Teacher's Guide to the Big Mathematical Ideas for Kindergartners

Number and Operations: Representing, Comparing, and Ordering Whole Numbers and Joining and Separating Sets

"Students use numbers, including written numerals, to represent quantities and solve quantitative problems, such as counting objects in a set; counting out a given number of objects; comparing sets or numerals; and modeling simple joining and separating situations with objects . . . Students choose, combine, and apply effective strategies for answering quantitative questions, including quickly recognizing the cardinalities of small sets of objects, counting and producing sets of given sizes, counting the number in combined sets, or counting the number of objects that remain in a set after some are taken away." (Common Core State Standards Initiative 2010)

Number Focus

(1) Cardinality, **(2)** Number Word List (*one, two, three, four, five,* etc.), **(3)** One-to-One Counting Correspondence, and **(4)** Written Numbers Symbols (*1, 2, 3,* etc.)

Breaking It Down

(1)   Cardinality: Teacher Look-Fors

Does the child subitize (instantly see) small quantities?

Teacher: How many dots do you see?
Child who subitizes: Three. (immediately)
Child not yet subitzing: One, two, three or One, two, three. There's three.

After counting objects in a set or creating a set with objects, does the child know that the last counting number said is the total of the set?

Child counts:

●   ●   ●   ●

"One,"   "two,"   "three,"   "four."
Teacher: So how many?
Child with sense of cardinality: Four.
Child without fully developed sense of cardinality: One, two, three, four.

---

(2) Number Word List (*one, two three, four, five,* etc.): Teacher Look-Fors

How high can the child orally count to?
  Teacher: What is the largest number you know? What is the highest number you can count to? Okay, go ahead and start counting from one.

Can the child begin counting orally from a number other than one?
  Teacher: Start counting at ten and see how far you can go. (*Does the child find the transition into eleven, twelve, and the teen numbers difficult without starting from one?*)

Does the child skip numbers at a certain point in the count?
  Skipping teen numbers is particularly common for many kindergartners. For those counting past twenty, skipping decades ("Thirty-seven, 38, 39, 50, 51, 52 . . .") is also common.

Does the pace of the counting slow at a certain point?
  The pace often slows at the point of difficulty (teen numbers, decade changes, etc).

Can the child count backward? From what number?

Can the child count by tens?

Ask yourself, "What is the next step for this child's counting?"

(continued)

Figure 6.2 A Teacher's Guide to the Big Mathematical Ideas for Kindergartners *(continued)*

---

(3) One-to-One Counting Correspondence: Teacher Look-Fors

When counting objects:

> Does the child say one number word for each object counted?
> Does the child organize the count to track which objects have been counted and which have not?
> Does the child tag each object once, without skipping or double-tagging?

See the section titled "Counting Collections Math Exchanges" in this chapter for more information on one-to-one-counting correspondence.

---

(4) Written Number Symbols (*1, 2, 3*, etc.): Teacher Look-Fors

Writing numerals is a much more difficult task than identifying and recognizing numerals.

> Is the child reversing numbers? This is fairly common and becomes easier with age and practice.

> Does the child have difficulty writing the teen numbers? Many children hear "nineteen" and write *91*. Because *nine* is the first part of the word *nineteen*, it makes sense that kindergartners would write the number nine first. Again, this is fairly common and can be corrected with discussion, time, and practice.

Numerical Relationships (More Than/Less Than) Focus

Identifying and understanding the relationship between two groups of objects or two numbers.

Does the child use strategies of counting and matching to determine which of two sets has more? Does the child begin to use the words *less* and *fewer* in describing similar sets?

Can the child use objects or drawings, matching and counting to find out which is more and which is less for sets of numbers less than or equal to ten?

Can the child solve "How many more?" problem-solving situations using counting and matching situations?

For more information on more than/less than numerical relationships in math exchanges, see the section titled "A Comparing Counting Collections Math Exchange" in this chapter.

Operations Focus

Problem solving using mainly addition and subtraction, although some informal multiplication and division may be included.

Does the child use objects, fingers, drawings, or counters to solve a variety of join and separate type problems with totals less than or equal to ten?

Can the child decompose three, four, five, and six? For more on decomposing and composing numbers, see the section titled "Developing the Five-Structure and Ten-Structure in Kindergarten" in this chapter.

Does the child view equations written in the following ways as equally valid: $2 + 4 = 6$ and $6 = 2 + 4$?

Adapted from Focus in Kindergarten: Teaching with Curriculum Focal Points *(Fuson, Clements, and Beckmann 2010)* and "Mathematics: Kindergarten: Introduction" *(Common Core State Standards Initiative 2010)*.

Counting Collections Math Exchanges

Counting a set of objects is one of the most important goals of kindergarten. While counting may seem like a simple skill for adults, counting for kindergartners involves a great deal of problem solving. In kindergarten many children are just starting to make the connection between quantities, counting words, and written numerals. Nevertheless, counting goes far beyond these initial ideas. In "Counting Collections," Julie Kern Schwerdtfeger and Angela Chan (2007) discuss the connections between counting collections of everyday items such as shells, rocks, and buttons and problem solving throughout the elementary grades. They believe that the counting of collections of items offers children "rich opportunities to practice oral counting, develop efficient counting strategies, group objects in strategic ways, record numbers, and represent their thinking" (356).

Counting collections is an excellent way to begin math exchanges in kindergarten. My students never tire of counting collections and ask to return to them during partner time throughout the year. And of course, there is an endless list of interesting items to be counted in our world, from beans and stones to school supplies like glue sticks and pencils.

Counting collections can provide a strong structure to your math workshop as you begin the year. Your math workshop can begin with count-around-the-circle warm-up routines and continue into counting centers or counting collection partners. Counting practice can be expanded upon during math exchanges and serve as a starting point for reflection. Reflection time is a great time for children to share counting strategies they used, counting challenges they ran across, and counting experiences they plan to explore next. Counting collections with partners is also a great community-building task. The talking, negotiation, compromise, and problem solving kids run into while counting a collection of objects with a partner establish a strong foundation of interdependence and cooperation in the classroom.

Let's take a look at how I structure two kinds of counting collection math exchanges in October for kindergartners: show-us counting collections and comparing counting collections.

A Show-Us Counting Collections Math Exchange

Martha, Brenda, and Javier sit down with me on the rug in the meeting area of the classroom. I have chosen this particular spot to work during math exchanges because it is separated from the rest of the kids working in centers, yet I am in a position where I can keep an eye on the goings-on of the math workshop. I can see one group of kids who are working with the instructional assistant on a math game from the *Investigations* curriculum. Two other groups are working in counting collection centers. At each of these centers there are numbered paper bags filled with interesting items to count. Some children work alone, while others work together counting and recording the contents of each bag. We have set out cafeteria trays so that each group can have a contained workspace in which to organize and count their collection. Finally, one other group of children is in the explore center building with blocks.

In order to devote planning time to thinking about next steps for children within math exchanges, it's a good idea to plan simple yet meaningful games and independent tasks centers. Your school's textbook series is often a good place to start when looking for meaningful games and tasks for students to work on during center time.

After scanning the classroom to see that the other students are focused and working, I return to the three kids sitting with me for our math exchange. "Let's warm up our brains a little bit!" I say to the group. I place a handful of large lima beans onto a tray in front of us. "There are a lot of lima beans in that handful, but you are not going to count them all. I'm going to give you each a number of lima beans to count out from the big pile here. Javier, show us six beans." Javier pulls beans from the pile and counts out six beans, placing them in a line. Martha and Brenda watch Javier carefully.

"That's six," says Javier, satisfied.

"What do you think?" I ask Martha and Brenda.

Martha touches each bean in Javier's row, recounting. "It's six," she confirms. Now it is Brenda's turn.

"Brenda, show us eight beans," I say. Brenda starts counting out beans and putting them in a row as Javier did. However, after five she starts counting quickly and loses her one-to-one correspondence, saying, "Six, seven," while only counting out one bean. She ends up with only seven beans in her collection. (See Figure 6.3.)

"What do you think?" I ask the group again.

"No, you count too quick," says Martha, recounting Brenda's group of beans.

Figure 6.3
Brenda's Counting

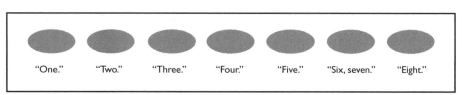

"One."   "Two."   "Three."   "Four."   "Five."   "Six, seven."   "Eight."

"Oh," laughs Brenda. "I need one more for eight," she says, adding another bean to her collection.

Next I ask Martha to count out five. She eagerly pulls beans from the pile. "One, two, three, four, five, six . . ."

"Stop!" says Javier. "That's too many." Martha, like many kindergartners, has not fully grasped the idea of cardinality, the idea that the last number said when counting represents the total number of beans. Sometimes when asked to count out a specific number of items from a group, she will simply continue counting as high as she can or until she has counted the whole group of available objects. Knowing when to stop the count is her challenge.

"What happened?" I ask curiously. Martha shrugs. She knows something is not quite right, but she is not sure how to correct for her error.

Javier shows us. "One, two, three, four, five, *stop!*" he says emphatically.

You may be wondering why I believe this kind of exchange is worthwhile. After all, I said very little during this short exchange. Couldn't I encourage these same ideas and guide the same conversations by walking around to the different centers? Certainly, it would be easier to do it that way.

This math exchange was worthwhile for two reasons. First, this kind of focused conversation, in which children are actively listening and responding to each other's ideas and actions, are most powerful in small groups. According to Fuson, Clements, and Beckmann, "Children are often better at seeing counting errors when other children make them" (2010, 3). Had we been at a center, the kids may have missed Brenda's counting error, being too busy and interested in their own counting pursuits. Second, counting math exchanges allow me to collect careful, authentic data on my students. I am able to efficiently record their progress with counting and note the kinds of counting errors they make. This allows me to better plan for future math exchanges and see trends within my classroom that may be best addressed as a whole group and through more independent or center-time practice.

The most obvious way to differentiate this kind of show-us math exchange to meet each child's needs is to vary the numbers. However, in order to give additional practice with number recognition and number writing, I may add these elements to the math exchange:

- Instead of having the kids show objects, ask them to show a number on their fingers. Then take note of who has to count each finger to show six; who automatically flashes the number on his or her fingers; who can show six a different way on his or her fingers; and who can self-correct by looking at a friend's fingers. Finger flashing can tell you a lot about a child's counting development and can begin conversations about different combinations that make a number, an important concept in kindergarten and beyond.

- Start the show-us exchange by giving each child a numeral card showing how many objects to count out. Ask them to identify the number.
- End the show-us exchange by providing a number line and saying, "You just counted five teddy bears. Can you show us which number is five on this number line?"
- End the show-us exchange by saying, "You just counted out five teddy bears. Can you record how you counted out and organized the bears? Remember, mathematicians sometimes use symbols like circles or *x*'s instead of drawing all the bears. You can also write the number five on your paper." (See Figures 6.4 and 6.5 for examples of how students might record their thinking for any counting collections math exchange.)
- Do you teach an older grade? Counting collections make for great mathematical experiences throughout the primary grades. Try giving students larger collections to count. How do children count larger collections? Do

Figure 6.4
Kyra represents her counting collection of eight snowmen with realistic drawings and keeps track of the total by writing the number above each snowman.

Figure 6.5
Mackayla represents her counting collection of ten snowmen with symbolic drawings and by writing only the total number of snowmen.

they group by fives, tens, or hundreds to help them keep track of the running total? Try giving children packs of items, such as several boxes of eight markers. How do they count the collection of markers without being able to touch each individual item?

A Comparing Counting Collections Math Exchange

Being able to describe and compare numbers and quantities is an important skill that kindergartners can begin to work on through counting collections math exchanges. (Figures 6.6a–c show students at work in counting collections math exchanges.)

Figures 6.6a–c
Children throughout the primary grades benefit from experiences with counting collections.

Nester, Calvin, and Jocelyn sit down in front of three cafeteria trays with paper bags on them. "Okay, friends, let's dump out our counting collections on our trays," I say. "Don't start counting yet though!"

The three kindergartners pour out their bags containing different numbers of pink pencil-top erasers.

"Oh!" say the kids excitedly, feeling the erasers between their fingers.

"These are squishy," laughs Nester.

"Let's look at our piles of erasers," I say. "Are all the erasers the same size?"

"Yes, but Calvin has more!" says Jocelyn.

"How do you know Calvin has more?" I ask.

"Cause his pile is the biggest," responds Jocelyn again.

"Oh, so sometimes we can tell who has more just by looking. Sometimes we don't need to count to see who has more," I say, responding to the idea that Jocelyn has brought up. "Calvin, do you think you have the *most* erasers?" I ask, pointing to his pile.

"Yes, I have the more [*sic*] erasers," replies Calvin, pointing to his own pile and then to the piles of his two friends.

"Calvin has the *most* erasers," I say, pointing to a place on the classroom wall where we've written the words *the most, the fewest, more, fewer*, and *the same*. The differences between these terms are difficult for many kindergartners, but I know they can grasp the concept, even if their verbal expressions of the concept are still approximations.

"What else do you notice about the erasers?" I ask.

"I have the little number," replies Nester.

"Nester's erasers is the little pile," adds Jocelyn, showing the size of the pile with her hands for emphasis.

"So, Nester has the *fewest* erasers," I reply. "Okay, let's count up those erasers to see just how many you each have." The kids each pull back slightly from the group with their cafeteria trays and begin counting. They want their own space to focus and not get distracted by the counting of the other group members. As the three kindergartners count their erasers I am looking for and jotting down some important information:

- Can the child compare different quantities of items before counting them? What kind of language does he or she use to compare the groups?
- Does the child have a system for keeping track of which items have been counted and which items still need to be counted?
- Does the child maintain one-to-one correspondence while counting or does he or she lose the one-to-one when counting larger collections?

- Does the child skip any count numbers or slow down or stop altogether after a certain number?
- Can the child report the last number counted as the total number of items in the group?
- Can the child recognize and/or write the numeral that corresponds to his or her total?

After the children have counted their collections (Calvin has twenty-one erasers, Nester eight, and Jocelyn fifteen) and we have identified the numerals and written them together, they can confirm or change their initial ideas about who has the *most* and the *fewest*.

"I was right! I have the more erasers!" shouts Calvin, still confusing *more* with *most*.

"How do we know Calvin has the *most* erasers?" I ask. I model correctly using the mathematical language, but accept his approximations as appropriate at this point in his linguistic and mathematical development.

"Because his number is twenty-one and my number is fifteen and Calvin's is eight. Twenty-one is the biggest number," explains Jocelyn.

"Yeah, eight is first, then after comes fifteen, and then after comes twenty-one," adds Nester, referring to the order in which the numbers are counted.

From this point in a math exchange like this one, I have several choices. In October, when we are just building our stamina and focus, I might choose to end the math exchange here, when the students have counted and compared their collections. Later in the year, depending on my goals for the group, we might continue to a story problem, such as one of the following:

Jocelyn has 15 erasers. Nester gives Jocelyn his 8 erasers. How many erasers does Jocelyn have now? (Join Result Unknown)

Calvin had 21 erasers. He gave 5 to Ms. Wedekind. How many erasers does Calvin have now? (Separate Result Unknown)

Nester has 8 erasers. Ms. Wedekind gives him some more. Now Nester has 10 erasers. How many erasers did Ms. Wedekind give to Nester? (Join Change Unknown)

Ms. Wedekind has some erasers hiding in her hand. Jocelyn gives Ms. Wedekind all of her 15 erasers. Now Ms. Wedekind has 20 erasers. How many erasers were hiding in Ms. Wedekind's hand in the beginning? (Join Start Unknown)

Nester has 15 erasers. Jocelyn has 8 erasers. How many more erasers does Nester have than Jocelyn? (Compare Difference Unknown)

Developing the Five-Structure and Ten-Structure in Kindergarten

The five-structure and, eventually, the ten-structure are big ideas for the kindergarten mathematician. "The essence of understanding 'five-ness' is understanding what the symbol 5 means and how five can be represented and visualized in different ways" (Novakowski 2007, 226). Because five and ten are such important numbers in our number system, developing a sense of five and ten plays a crucial role in developing solid number sense from an early age. NCTM's *Principles and Standards for School Mathematics* states that in prekindergarten through second grade teachers should focus on providing experiences and instruction that encourage students to do the following:

- *Develop a sense of whole numbers and represent and use them in flexible ways, including relating, composing, and decomposing numbers*
- *Connect number words and numerals to the quantities they represent, using various physical models and representations* [see Figure 6.7] (NCTM 2011c)

Figure 6.7
Number Word, Numeral, and Quantity Connection for Five

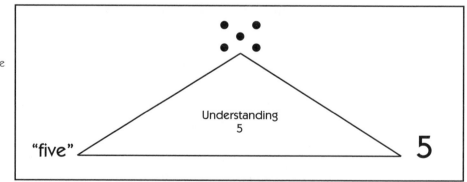

Developing an understanding of the five-structure is a goal attainable by kindergartners. In my experience, most kindergartners can begin extending this knowledge to ten, but strengthen the understanding of ten in first and second grade.

Math Exchanges That Encourage Understanding of "Five-ness"

As kindergarten students begin their work in centers (some very simple, independent centers and one game center run by her instructional assistant), their teacher, Michelle Gale, calls two or three students at a time to sit on the rug with her away from the hustle and bustle of the rest of the math workshop. Michelle finds two to four students to be the optimal number for kindergarten math exchanges. Her kindergarten math exchanges usually last from five to ten minutes—just long enough to tell and retell a story problem, give time for independent solving, and have a brief reflection in which children learn to compare and contrast their strategies with those of the other group members.

Today the kindergartners are exploring the idea of composing and decomposing five using an open part-part-whole problem.

"We have a bunch of red and blue crayons in our crayon tub," Michelle says as she shows the group a tub of red and blue crayons. "I want to give everyone in the class five crayons, but I want to know all the different ways that I could give them five red and blue crayons. What is one way that you think I could do this?"

Javier looks to his fingers. He knows he has five fingers on one hand and he is lifting and lowering fingers as he makes sense of the problem in his mind. After a few moments he responds, "I think one red crayon and four blue crayons."

"Let's try out Javier's idea," Michelle responds, without giving feedback as to whether this is a correct or incorrect answer. "Use the blue and red crayons or the blue and red Unifix cubes to help you check Javier's idea. Can you tell us what your idea was one more time, Javier?"

More confidently this time, Javier replies, "One red and four blues is five."

Jocelyn gets out the crayons that Javier had named. Calvin uses the Unifix cubes, connecting one red with four blues, and then counting them all again to make sure he has five crayons.

"So, we know that one red crayon and four blue crayons is one way to solve this problem. Are there other ways that I could give five blue and red crayons to kids?" Michelle asks.

"All blue," Jocelyn responds. "Five blue crayons and no red crayons." Calvin and Javier nod their heads in response to Jocelyn's idea.

"Is there another way, Calvin?" Michelle asks.

"Five red and five blue?" Calvin responds, unsure. This is a common mistake in part-part-whole problems—students often misinterpret the whole for the number required of each part.

"Show us," Michelle requests, gesturing to the Unifix cubes that Calvin used earlier in this exchange. Calvin gets out five red cubes and five blue ones, connecting them into a long train. "So, if I give you five red crayons *and* five blue crayons, do you have five crayons altogether?" Michelle continues.

"No!" exclaims Jocelyn. "That's ten."

"Too many?" Calvin offers.

"That's too many. You can only have five," adds Javier. Calvin removes the five blue cubes from his train and recounts the red ones. He offers the remaining five red cubes up to the group for consideration. "Five."

While the three kindergartners in this math exchange are at different levels of understanding part-part-whole relationships, Michelle feels that they are ready to start experimenting further with this problem. With a few more comments on this problem, the kids are off trying to find as many combinations of red and blue crayons totaling five as they can. Because this is the first time these kindergartners have worked on this kind of problem, Michelle does not ask them to record their combinations of five and does not question them as to when they know they have all the combinations. In fact, many kids repeat the same combination several times without realizing it.

Michelle repeats this math exchange, adjusting the questioning according to the group over the next couple of days. When all of the kids have had a chance to work in math exchanges, Michelle takes the opportunity to bring all of the groups together to do a whole-class reflection. In this case, all children have had the opportunity to experience a very similar math exchange, and Michelle believes that having them reflect and record their ideas as a whole group aids them in solidifying ideas.

In reflecting, whether as a whole group or during a math exchange, Michelle and I have found that it is important to have the tools and manipulatives available to the children who are sharing their strategies. This is especially important in a school with many English language learners, where the ability to explain a strategy verbally may lag behind the ability of a kindergartner to show you what he or she has done. As the children report their ideas about the crayon problem, using crayons or Unifix cubes to explain their thinking, Michelle records their thinking on chart paper. Though she records the ideas as they are shared, she strategically writes them in a certain order that she believes will help children see that they have exhausted the combinations of five (see Figure 6.8).

As she records the ideas, Michelle asks questions to push her students' thinking: "Do you notice anything interesting happening with the numbers?" "How do you know if you've found all the different combinations?" Michelle

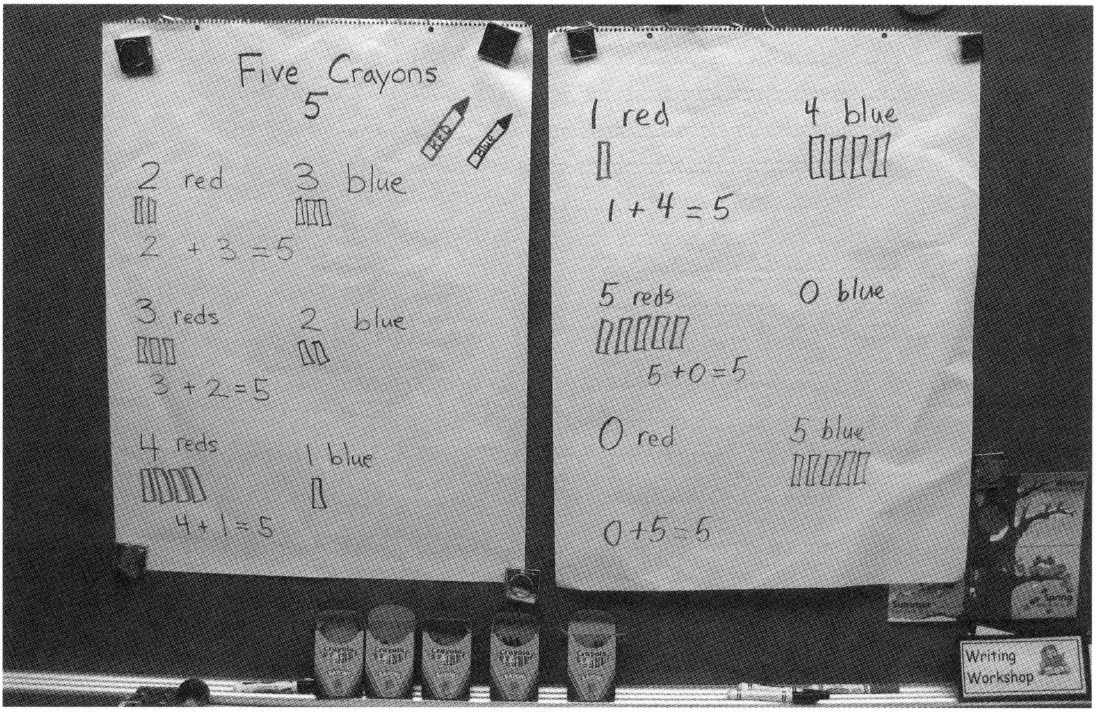

Figure 6.8 Michelle charts her students' ideas from the crayon problem.

wonders if some of her students notice the compensation she is highlighting by the order in which she records the ideas.

Halla is ready to start thinking about these ideas. "I started with five red crayons," she explains. "All red. Then I take away one red and put in one blue. Then I take away another red crayon and put in another blue. And again and again until they're all blue." Michelle uses pictorial and numerical representations and writes the corresponding equation to record the idea that Halla brings up. A couple of other kids echo and add on to Halla's ideas. They're all at different points in their understanding, but all have gotten something out of this problem-solving task.

Over the next few days Michelle gives the children another similar task in small-group math exchanges:

> Six hamsters live in two connected cages, one purple and one black. The
> hamsters like to run back and forth between the purple cage and the black cage.
> Show all the different combinations of hamsters that could be in the purple and
> black cages.

This time Michelle provides Unifix cubes, markers, pens, and paper for the children to work on the problem. Many children refer to the crayon chart to help them organize their work. Once again, the children gather together to share their work, focusing their conversation on decomposing and composing six, and recording their ideas in a way that makes sense to others.

Try It Out!

Working with Five

Michelle often uses a five-frame to help her students learn combinations of five (see Figure 6.9). As a warm-up in her math exchanges, she flashes five-frames with between zero and five colored dots. After showing the kids the five-frame for about two seconds, Michelle hides the frame and asks:

- *How many dots did you see?*
- *How many more dots do we need to make five/fill the five-frame?*

Use Join Change Unknown problems such as the following to build children's ability to decompose and compose the number five:

I have 3 pretzels. I wish I had 5. How many more do I need to have 5?

Figure 6.9
Kindergarten teacher Lauren Nye uses a five-frame to help her students learn combinations of five.

Math Exchanges That Encourage Understanding of "Ten-ness"

In addition to needing many opportunities to explore the five-structure, kindergartners are also ready to begin exploring the most important number in our number system, ten. While full understanding of ten is more complex than five and will certainly continue into first grade, kindergartners at various points in their journey toward numeracy are ready to work toward an understanding of ten.

Any kind of problem type can be used when focusing on representing, visualizing, decomposing, and composing the number ten.

One morning Michelle Gale and I decided to use the day's math exchanges as an informal formative assessment with a Separate Result Unknown (SRU) problem to get a better idea of how the kids were problem solving with ten. We used this problem:

> During the big snowstorm, Cruz and Calvin made 10 snowmen—some in the sun and some in the shade. The two snowmen in the sun melted. How many snowmen were left in the shade?

Before the kids came in that morning, Michelle and I sat down briefly to talk about what strategies we expected to see. We quickly recorded the strategies in a chart (Figure 6.10) as we talked and used the chart to collect data as we worked in math exchanges over the next couple of days. We found that some of the students used direct modeling to solve the problem and some were beginning to bridge modeling and counting strategies.

Shades of Difference Among Direct Modelers: Jocelyn, Nester, and Javier

Many kindergartners stay within the realm of direct modeling strategies throughout their kindergarten year. And yet, not all modeling strategies are created equal. In fact, different children using modeling strategies may actually have very different levels of understanding that need to be explored in order for the teacher to responsively guide instruction both within and outside of math exchanges.

Let's take a look at some of the kindergartners' strategies for solving the snowmen problem in order to get an idea of how diverse children's thinking and modeling strategies can be.

Figure 6.10 Spreadsheet of Strategies: Separate Result Unknown (SRU)

Date: _January 13, 2010_

During the big snowstorm Cruz and Calvin made 10 snowmen—some in the sun and some in the shade. The two snowmen in the sun melted. How many snowmen were left in the shade?

Student Name	Modeling Strategy	Counting Strategy	Facts Strategy	Notes
Jocelyn	✓			Modeled w/ cubes first. Counted out 10, removed 2, counted remaining from 1. Then drew snowmen as another way to represent.
Nester	✓			Put up 10 fingers. Put down 2. Counted on from 5.
Javier	✓		✓	Javier drew a full ten-frame, marking each line as having 5. Crossed off 2, and saw 4 + 4 = 8 in his ten-frame. Wrote 8.
Hannah		✓		Counted 2 back from 10 to land on 8. Later represented in various ways. Told me that 5 + 5 = 10 helped her.
Diego		✓		Counted 2 back from 10 to land on 8 in his head. Only recorded numbers. Used 5 + 5 = 10 to help him.
Brenda	✓			Drew 10 snowmen. Crossed off 2 and recounted from 1 for total. Wrote 8. Also recorded "5 5 10."
Halla	✓		✓	Drew snowmen in ten-structure. Crossed 2 off. Then said, "Eight, because 4 plus 4 equals 8." Wrote "5 + 5 = 10" and "10 − 2 = 8."
Mackayla		✓ (incorrect: 7)		Put up 10 fingers. Put down 3 instead of 2. Counted on from 5.
Evelyn		✓		Counted back 2 from 10 to land on 8. Recorded "10 = 8 − 2 = 8." Then added drawing.

Jocelyn

Jocelyn is a classic direct modeler. To solve the snowmen problem she first used Unifix cubes to represent the ten snowmen, and then took away two cubes and counted from one to figure out the remaining number of snowmen. When I asked Jocelyn to explain to me how she solved the problem, she simply re-created her model with cubes and solved the problem again. Later, Jocelyn represented her strategy on paper with the drawing shown in Figure 6.11. Within the context of this story problem, Jocelyn was not yet thinking of ten as a special number. She didn't yet know combinations of ten that would help her solve this problem.

Figure 6.11
Jocelyn's
Snowmen Problem

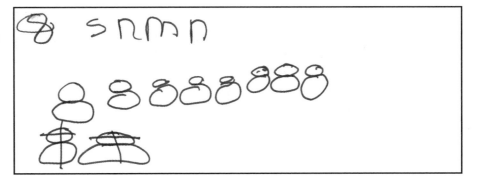

Nester

Nester also used a modeling strategy to solve the snowmen problem. He showed ten with his fingers, dropped two fingers, and counted on from five to determine how many fingers were remaining. (See Nester's drawing in Figure 6.12.) However, when Nester explained his strategy, he alluded to a beginning understanding of the ten-structure.

Figure 6.12
Nester's Snowmen
Problem

"So, Nester, I saw you using your fingers to figure the problem out. Tell me what you did," I probed.

"I know I have five fingers and five fingers, so ten fingers," Nester responded, gesturing to his hands. "I take two fingers from one hand of five fingers, so there's three fingers on the hand. So, five, six, seven, eight. Eight snowmen."

So, how did Nester's understanding of ten differ from Jocelyn's? They both modeled the problem using objects (Jocelyn with the cubes and Nester with his fingers). However, Nester began solving this problem by using his understanding of 5 fingers + 5 fingers = 10 fingers to begin breaking this problem down. He was beginning to see his five fingers on one hand as a unit that could be decomposed in order to solve the problem more easily.

Notice that even though both Jocelyn and Nester used strategies that were easy for Michelle and me to understand, we still asked them to explain their strategies. Not only does this provide the children practice for being able to explain and reflect upon one's strategy from an early age, but it provided us with extra insight into Nester's thinking that we may not have noticed had we not asked.

Javier

Javier showed some similarities in his understanding of ten to that of Nester. Javier was also thinking about ten as two groups of five, which he demonstrated by drawing a full ten-frame to represent the ten snowmen in the problem (see Figure 6.13). Around the time when Michelle and I gave this problem, the class had been doing a lot of work with ten-frames, both as visual quick-image warm-ups and as a tool for problem solving. After Javier solved the problem, I commented, "Javier, I notice that you drew a ten-frame. How did that help you understand this problem?"

Figure 6.13
Javier's Snowmen
Problem

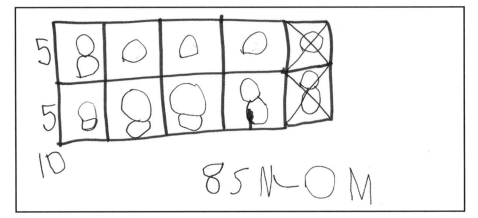

"I think in my mind of all ten boxes full of snowmans," Javier explained. "Then I take two away, and I saw four and four left. Four plus four equals eight."

"Oh, so you used the ten-frame to help you think about what you know about five plus five and four plus four. That's a strong strategy," I respond.

Javier was also a direct modeler. He still needed to create the ten snowmen and remove two snowmen to solve the problem. However, his creation of the ten-frame allowed Javier to access facts he already knew ($5 + 5 = 10$ and $4 + 4 = 8$) to help solve the problem.

Bridging Modeling and Counting Strategies: Hannah and Diego

Looking at Hannah and Diego's work, we see lingering elements of modeling strategies. In fact, Hannah created a drawing model for the problem *after* solving the problem with her original, more efficient strategy. This is important to note. Sometimes kindergartners are so comfortable using modeling strategies to solve problems that they hold on to them for a while even when the model they create no longer represents how they are actually conceptualizing the problem. One way to work with students you think are ready to move away from modeling strategies toward counting strategies is to tell the story orally and have students respond with their strategies orally rather than recording them on paper.

Hannah

Hannah's first strategy was a counting one. "I know five plus five is ten. Then I count back two. Ten, nine, eight," she explained to me, using her fingers to keep track of the jumps backward. However, even though Hannah was confident in her strategy, she still went on to create a model of the story with her drawing (see Figure 6.14). As Hannah finished her snowmen drawing, she added offhandedly, "Oh, and I could also show it this way," as she drew an open number line representing her thinking. This kind of model is one I had shown the class before when creating a visual representation of students' thinking, but I had never seen Hannah create an open number line herself. Hannah was clearly experimenting with different ways of representing her thinking.

Once, I asked Hannah about another problem, which she had also solved with a counting strategy: "Do you need to do all those cat drawings to figure out the problem?"

"No," she told me matter-of-factly. "Sometimes I just like to draw cats. And I can also make *sure* I'm right when I draw *all twenty* of the cats."

Figure 6.14
Hannah's
Snowmen Problem

Hannah has summed it up for us. Even kindergartners ready for counting strategies may hold on to their modeling strategies both as a way of checking their newfound counting strategies and because, to the kindergarten mind, drawing twenty cats might seem like a fun task rather than an arduous one. That's okay. In kindergarten there may be a great disparity between the actual strategy the child uses to solve a problem and what the child records. While I believe learning how to record one's thinking is important in kindergarten, this means that the conversations during math exchanges are even more important, as students clarify both their thinking and what they have chosen to record.

Diego
Diego, on the other hand, was confident in the counting back strategies he had been using recently. He explained his work, pointing to the numbers and words he had recorded: "Five plus five is ten. Take away two that melted. Nine, eight snowmen." Someone who just looks at Diego's work in Figure 6.15 may think his simple recording means that his strategy was also not very sophisticated. However, in knowing and talking with Diego, we realized that Diego's recording matched pretty closely to his thinking. He didn't add superfluous details to what he recorded, and he did not yet know how to record his ideas in the form of an equation, but he had a sophisticated strategy for solving this problem.

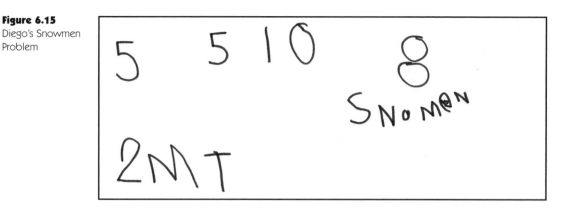

Figure 6.15
Diego's Snowmen
Problem

❖❖❖

Some teachers have asked me how verbal discussion of strategies works with children just learning English. Five of the six students discussed in this section were English language learners who spoke only Spanish at home and whose first experiences with English were in the fall of their kindergarten year. In the beginning of the year, their strategy explanation was more a matter of showing than telling. However, with daily practice talking about problem solving and the use of some of the scaffolds for strategy talk discussed earlier in this chapter, they were successfully able to communicate their thinking in English through a combination of showing and telling.

Try It Out!

Working with Ten

At our school, one of my roles as math coach is that of the Queen of Ten (see Figure 6.16). Every ten days of school, the Queen visits kindergarten classes to lead the kids in a celebratory task involving the number ten. Whether or not you have a Queen of Ten at your school, you can introduce some of these tasks in your math exchanges:

- *The Queen's Wand.* One important element of the Queen of Ten's apparel is her wand. The wand is made of ten Unifix cubes, five of one color connected to five of another color. Having your students build wands for the Queen can be a great independent task to help build understanding of the five-structure's relationship to ten.
- *Broken Wand!* This is a warm-up I use during the first minute or two of many math exchanges focusing on the ten-structure. It can also be used

as a whole-group warm-up or as a game played with partners. After children have experience with what the Queen's wand looks like, I hide the wand behind my back and break it into two pieces. I show the children one part of the wand. Using their knowledge of the five-structure, children tell me how many cubes are missing from the Queen's wand. Here are some questions I use for this warm-up:

What do we know about the Queen's wand? (This allows kids to verbalize and remind themselves that the wand is constructed from five Unifix cubes of one color and five Unifix cubes of another color.)
How many cubes does this broken wand have? How do you know?
How many cubes are missing from the wand? How many more cubes does the wand need to have ten cubes? How do you know?

Figure 6.16 The Queen of Ten (me!) makes a visit to a kindergarten class.

Multiplication and Division with Kindergartners

As I mentioned in Chapter 4, multiplication and division are not usually associated with kindergartners. Yet, multiplication and division story problems often come naturally to kindergartners, because they are quite easy to model. Also, if the teacher chooses strategic numbers for the story problems, such as two, five, or ten, children who are ready will begin to apply skip-counting strategies to multiplication and division problems.

Let's take a look at a math exchange with a group of kindergartners.

"I want to share a problem with you today about some children who are eating snack," I tell the group.

"Just like us. Is it time for snack now?" asks Jocelyn.

"Not yet. It's math time," replies the ever-serious Chris.

"Sometimes you all eat crackers for snack," I say, "and that is what the kids are eating in this story. Let's listen to the story."

6 friends are eating snack. They each eat 2 crackers. How many crackers did the friends eat altogether?

As we go through the process of retelling the story I hold up a simple drawing of a child and record the numeral *6* above it when the children tell me there are six friends in the story. After I show the picture of a cracker, I ask Halla to record the numeral *2* above it. Not only does this technique provide a visual reference for the many English language learners at our school but also it gives the children practice associating the numeral with the spoken number and, eventually, the quantity, once they begin to solve the problems. In the beginning of the year, I may model the writing of the numeral; in the middle of the year the children record together; and by the end of the kindergarten year most children are able to record independently the numbers that we use in problem solving.

After I have read the snack story, Chris yells excitedly, "I know how to do this!" Indeed, Chris's work (see Figure 6.17) illustrates that he clearly understands the problem. Chris draws six people and draws groups of two crackers,

Figure 6.17
Chris's Cracker
Problem

with arrows pointing from each cracker group to the person to whom they belong. However, because Chris's ability to illustrate his strategy lags developmentally behind his mathematical ideas, he gets confused with his drawing and gets an answer of eight.

Halla uses the same strategy as Chris, and with the help of more developed drawing skills, she gets an answer of twelve.

Jocelyn is hesitant about this problem. Six people sounds like a lot to her. After giving her some thinking time, I suggest, "What if there were only two people and they each ate two crackers. How many crackers would they eat altogether?" Jocelyn creates two groups of Unifix cubes and counts them, "One, two, three, four." She then reaches for paper to record her answer with a drawing, as she has seen Chris and Halla do.

Hannah is the only student who uses a more sophisticated modeling strategy. Rather than draw people, she uses numerals to represent the six people and two tally marks beneath each numeral to represent the crackers (see Figure 6.18). Then she counts all the tally marks and arrives at twelve as her answer. Hannah has been practicing skip-counting throughout math workshop, and she is close to being able to apply this skill to problem solving by counting her tally marks by twos, or simply by labeling the crackers by twos with numerals. I make a note to focus on this in my next math exchange with Hannah.

When the group has finished thinking and recording, Chris is adamant that his answer of eight is correct. "Look," he says to the group, pointing to this picture. "I made six people and they all have two crackers and that's what the story told us."

Halla, Jocelyn, and Hannah look at Chris's drawing. It looks similar to what they did, but they aren't sure why he has a different answer.

Figure 6.18
Hannah's Cracker Problem

I don't confirm or correct anyone's answer at this point. I simply ask for more proof. "Chris, could you show us your strategy, but this time use the Unifix cubes to show us?"

Chris makes groups of two Unifix cubes, saying, "This is one person, this is two people, this is three people, this is four people, this is five people, this is six people," to keep track of the groups. He starts counting from one and this time arrives at twelve.

"Oh, I guess it is twelve."

Halla points to Chris's drawing. "You forgot the crackers for some people."

"Oh, so maybe that is why he got a different answer the first time. I think Chris showed us something important though," I say. "Mathematicians check their work. Most of you used drawings to solve this problem. We think the friends ate twelve crackers altogether. Let's check that answer using another way to solve the problem."

The four children in this group are diverse in their mathematical understanding. Some children with whom I solve this problem are only solid with counting to ten. I know twelve will be a good stretch for them, so I may have to remind them of the names of the numbers after ten. Others cannot yet write the numbers up to ten. They may figure the problem out on their own using a number line to count to twelve and record the numeral they land on. They may orally tell me and then look to a friend for help for how to write it. I may model writing *12* for them and then have them write the number themselves. As I did with one child in this math exchange, I know I may need to lower the numbers to help some children gain the confidence to try the problem. And yet, *all* of the children in the class are ready to problem solve. Unfortunately, problem solving in kindergarten is sometimes reserved for only "high-achieving" students or is not done at all until the end of the kindergarten year. Counting, recognizing quantities, and writing numerals are all critical parts of the kindergarten mathematical experience. However, these skills can be embedded within problem solving as well as taught in more traditional ways.

Notice that in the math exchanges I have described (and in the examples that follow), I never used the terms *multiplication* and *division* or introduced number sentences such as $6 \times 2 = 12$. This is not the goal of a kindergarten math exchange focused on multiplication or division problem types. Nevertheless, these problem types provide experiences for kindergartners to start thinking about the ideas of grouping and partitioning—big ideas that will serve them as they continue to develop as problem solvers throughout their lives.

Try It Out!

Multiplication and Division Story Problems

Try some of these multiplication and division story problems that Michelle's kids worked on:

> Our class made gingerbread men to decorate. Phong made _____ gingerbread men. If each gingerbread man has 2 eyes, how many eyes in all did Phong put on his gingerbread men? (Multiplication Problem)

> Kayla wants to make some snowmen. To make a snowman she needs 2 snowballs. How many snowmen can Kayla make with 14 snowballs? (Division Problem)

> Mrs. Gale's class planted pumpkin seeds in the garden. They planted three rows of 5 seeds and one row of 3 seeds. How many seeds did Mrs. Gale's class plant? (Multiplication/Multistep Problem)

Young Children as Storytellers

Last summer several kindergarten teachers and I visited incoming kindergartners in their homes. Our goal was to talk with families about how they could introduce their child to many mathematical ideas through simply highlighting everyday situations—asking the child to count out enough forks for everyone in the house at dinner time, counting the stairs up to their apartment, telling funny math stories about the child's favorite animal.

One evening in August I visited the basement apartment of a family who lives just around the corner from our school. "I'm Frank! And you're the teacher! And I'm five," Frank informed me as he opened the door to his apartment to let me in. As I walked into Frank's apartment I was not surprised to see about ten adults crowded into the tiny living room. Many neighborhood families from our school share small apartments with relatives or even other unrelated families in order to afford the rent. However, I was surprised to find out that everyone in this living room was here to watch Frank meet the teacher. Frank's parents, uncles, aunts, and older sisters who lived with their own families had made a point to be at the apartment during our home visit.

It was certainly a home visit not to be forgotten—choral counting with the whole family, ten people playing a dice game on the living room floor, and talking about the family horse back in El Salvador (Frank's choice of a subject for our story problems). After about ten minutes of these tasks, I told Frank some story problems (*If everyone in this room wants to ride a horse, how many horses will we need? Frank has five horses in a barn. He forgets to close the barn door and two horses run away. How many are still in the barn?*), and then I asked Frank if he would like to tell me a story.

Not a shy boy, Frank launched into a story about chickens—another subject about which he obviously had some background knowledge. "There are ten chickens. Then two more eggs come out of the chicken and open up."

This was Frank's math story. While he was still developing the structure of a story problem, his ability to come up with this story on the spot was impressive.

As we were wrapping up the home visit, Frank's mom thanked me for coming. "We don't know a lot about math. But we can do what you did." Frank's mom may have thought she didn't know a lot of math, but she was obviously already empowering her son with substantial mathematical knowledge that he could take to kindergarten with him in the fall. More than just helping his family understand the math a kindergartner can do, this home visit with all of Frank's family present served the purpose of showing Frank how much his family valued learning and school.

Frank's older sister continued, "Frank has always talked and talked and talked since he was a baby. He loves to learn new things, so we keep answering questions, questions, and more questions."

"Exactly," I replied. "I think I could learn something from you about teaching math!"

As I left, I wondered what made Frank different from many of the other kids in his neighborhood. Frank's family had little education. Frank did not have the advantage of going to preschool. Yet his problem-solving abilities rivaled many children I visited who had these and many more advantages.

I think the answer lies in what Frank's older sister told me. Frank loved to talk, to tell stories. And so, taking their lead from Frank, they kept talking with him, kept telling him stories. In fact, I learned during the home visit that Frank, born in the United States himself, had never met the horse in El Salvador about which he had fondly told me in great detail. He knew of this horse only through the stories of his parents and older siblings!

Young children are both natural storytellers and natural mathematicians. Problem solving, as I have said before, is an exchange. So, what could be more natural an exchange than trading stories? Writing and posing story problems is an easy fit in the life of a kindergartner. As Outhred and Sardelich (2005) point out, "Problem posing is an open-ended activity that can be a powerful assessment tool because it reveals children's understanding of problem structure" (147).

So, how do you promote problem *posing* as well as problem solving throughout the math workshop? You start in a problem-posing math exchange!

Problem-Posing Math Exchanges

As the year progresses and kindergartners build more stamina for math exchanges, I often ask them, after they have solved one of my story problems, "Who wants to tell us your very own story problem?" There is usually no shortage of volunteers from the group. Let's look again at the story problem Frank told me when I was visiting his home:

There are ten chickens. Then two more eggs come out of the chicken and open up.

What does Frank's story tell us?

- "There are ten chickens . . ." Frank knows that many stories have a beginning that gives us information.
- "Then two more eggs come out of the chicken and open up." Frank knows that stories involve change to the status quo. In this case, Frank is implying a join problem by telling us how two more eggs (soon to be chickens when they open up) enter into the story.

What is Frank's story missing?

- The most obvious part of a story problem that is missing from Frank's story is the question, "How many chickens are there now?" When I asked Frank if this was what he wanted me to figure out, he quickly confirmed that indeed it was, but seemed baffled at why I needed to confirm this. Contrary to what might seem obvious to adults, not asking a question when problem posing is very common for children throughout elementary school. To children, the question seems to be implicit, even if it is not clear to adults what element of the story is to be solved.

Try It Out!

Math Storytelling

Children love hearing and telling stories. Introducing a mathematical element to the storytelling is most likely a natural fit to what you are already doing in your class.

- With your whole class, try a focus lesson on telling your own story. Make a class chart titled "How to Write a Story Problem" so that children can refer to the ideas they brainstormed to help them as they tell and write their own story problems.
- During a math exchange, ask a child to pose a problem to the group. For example, if you've just taken a field trip to the zoo, you may want to ask the child to tell a story about the trip to the zoo in order to help him or her focus on the content of the story.
- Ask the other children in the math exchange to retell the storyteller's problem. As the teacher, you can use this language to help facilitate the exchange:

  Who understands Kara's story?

  Does anyone have a question for Kara that would help you understand her story better?

  Does Kara's story include the important parts of our "How to Write a Story Problem" chart?

Although a problem-posing math exchange might be extended to a problem-solving math exchange, the focus of this kind of math exchange is on internalizing the structure of story problems. The more involved children are in creating meaning in their own stories, the better they become in finding meaning in the stories of others.

❖❖❖

If you are a kindergarten teacher, you already know that kindergarten is a time and place of amazing change and growth. Kindergartners are indeed extremely capable mathematicians. Imagine if, at the end of the school year, all kindergartners left understanding math as a medium through which to wonder about and investigate their world. Imagine if each child left kindergarten with a sense of ownership and agency in the world of mathematics. Imagine if all kindergartners viewed mathematics as place for play, creativity, and imagination. Imagine the possibilities for these young mathematicians. Endless.

Building Number Sense Through an Understanding of Ten

WHEN YOU THINK ABOUT THE FACT that people around the world communicate in thousands of languages, it is quite a marvel that our present base ten number system is used almost universally by modern societies. However, this has not always been the case. There is evidence of humans using tallies or slashes in bone, wood, and stone to record "how many" over 30,000 years ago (Devlin 2005). Of course, the effectiveness and efficiency of such a system of recording can only be sustained when the quantity being tracked is relatively small. As the need for a system of keeping track of money, trade, livestock, and important events expanded, so did the need for an efficient number system for dealing with large numbers. The base ten number system, initially developed by the Hindus over two thousand years ago, was introduced to the West by seventh-century Arabic mathematicians (Devlin 2000).

Understanding Our Number System

The Hindu-Arabic (base ten) number system was more efficient than previous number systems. Imagine how much more difficult writing, saying, and manipulating numbers would be if we used the Roman numeral system. MMMMDXCVIII is much more difficult to work with than 4,598. Unlike other number systems, the Hindu-Arabic number system draws on humans' early mathematical connection to using our ten fingers for counting. Interestingly, the same region of the brain that is most active when a person is doing arithmetic, the left partial lobe, is also the part of the brain most active in controlling finger movement—for activities such as counting! Mathematician Keith Devlin believes that this is "a consequence of the fact that counting began (with our early ancestors) as finger-enumeration, and that, over time, the human brain acquired the ability to 'disconnect' the fingers and perform the counting without physically manipulating them" (Devlin 2005, 204–205).

I have to admit that when I first became interested in how children learn mathematics, I gave little thought to the influence of our number system on the development of children's mathematical understanding. But when you consider how long it took humans to come up with and agree upon our modern base ten system, it is no surprise that this system is incredibly complex for children to construct in their own minds.

Although we pass down to children conventions such as how to form numerals and write number sentences, actual understanding must be constructed in the mind of the child. Constance Kamii asserts "that children acquire [mathematics] by *constructing* (making) it from the inside, in interaction with the environment, not by *internalizing* it from the outside through social transmission" (1994, 3). In other words, it is not enough just to explain a mathematical concept to children and have them practice the concept. This might produce results that mimic understanding, but it does not produce deep understanding and the ability to "think flexibly about numbers and construct a network of numerical relationships" (Kamii 2000, 69).

The building of "a network of numerical relationships" is not a linear process. Children make connections at different points in their mathematical careers, regardless of age or grade. This is not to say that we should simply wait and hope that children will construct these networks on their own. Yes, the networks of understanding must be built within the mind of the child. However, the role of the teacher is critical. The math exchanges a teacher plans can guide children toward making connections and building their mathematical understanding.

Research on Children's Understanding of Ten

Constructing a true understanding of the base ten system and place value is an incredibly complex process that develops slowly for many children, even with excellent instruction. Most first- and second-grade curricula focus on teaching place value through bundling groups of ten straws or sticks and the use of base ten blocks to illustrate that numbers are constructed out of tens and ones (e.g., 52 is made up of 5 tens and 2 ones). In past years, I, myself, have used many such instructional tools when teaching place value. In fact, I thought I was doing a pretty good job of teaching place value. Unfortunately, my students' understanding was often only surface level. Many had memorized a pattern that held little true meaning for them. The rote memorization discouraged the flexible thinking that would produce mathematicians with strong number sense and efficient strategies for computation.

The problem with such tasks as bundling straws and using base ten blocks is that they reinforce the idea that the digit 5 in 52 can only be viewed as five groups of ten. On the contrary, we want children to understand that the 5 digit in 52 is *simultaneously* fifty groups of one and five groups of ten. Furthermore, 52 can look like four groups of ten and twelve groups of one—and many, many other combinations. This kind of understanding builds flexible thinking and sets the stage for decomposing numbers for efficient computation down the road.

However, many children in first and second grade still struggle with the idea that ten is simultaneously ten ones and one ten. In studies published by Constance Kamii (including some research done by Mieko Kamii), children were asked to count and draw a group of sixteen chips. After writing *16*, the children were asked to identify what "this part" meant when the researcher pointed to the digit *6* and what "this part" meant when the researcher pointed to the digit *1* (Kamii 2000).

In Mieko Kamii's study, "the proportion of children who thought the '1' in '16' meant *ten* was 13% at age seven, 18% at age eight, and 42% at age nine" (Kamii 2000, 79). In Constance Kamii's subsequent study of older children, only 51 percent of fourth graders, 60 percent of sixth graders, and 78 percent of eighth graders responded that the *1* in *16* meant ten (Kamii 2000, 81).

In later experiments, researcher Sharon Ross conducted individual interviews with children in grades two through five. The sixty children in her research study were randomly selected children from thirty-three classrooms from rural, public, and private schools in Butte County, California (Ross 1986, 1990).

The first task in Ross's study asked children to build the number *52* using base ten blocks. Ross built a constraint into her experiment by having only 40 ones cubes available to the child so that the child could not build 52 through the exclusive use of ones cubes (Ross 1996, 1990).

Ross classified her results by three levels of performance, which are illustrated in Figure 7.1.

Figure 7.1 Results from the First Task in Ross's Study

Grade	Performance (n = 15 children per grade)		
	Level 1	Level 2	Level 3
2	5	1	9
3	0	3	12
4	1	1	13
5	0	1	14
Total	6	6	48

Level 1: The child was unsuccessful in building 52.
Level 2: The child first attempted to build 52 using ones cubes. When the child realized this was impossible with the materials provided, he or she eventually solved the problem using some of the tens blocks.
Level 3: The child quickly used 5 tens blocks and 2 ones cubes to build 52.

Adapted from Kamii 1994, 13.

Figure 7.2 Results from the Second Task in Ross's Study

Grade	Performance (n = 15 children per grade, 4 of whom did not attempt this task)		
	Level 1	Level 2	Level 3
2	5	4	2
3	2	5	8
4	1	5	9
5	0	4	11
Total	8	18	30

Level 1: The child was not successful.
Level 2: The child first attempted to build 52 using ones cubes. When the child realized this was impossible with the materials provided, he or she eventually solved the problem using some of the tens blocks. Sometimes the interviewer used a prompt, such as "Could you use some of these blocks?" to encourage students to use the tens blocks.
Level 3: The child was able to build 52 "another way." Common strategies included building 40 using 4 tens blocks and counting up to 52 using ones cubes, or trading 1 ten from the previous task in which the child built 52 using 5 tens and 2 ones, so that the child ended up with 4 tens and 12 ones.

Adapted from Kamii 1994, 15.

The second task in Ross's study asked children who had succeeded in building 52 in the previous task to find another way to build 52 using the base ten blocks. Again, Ross summarized children's performance into three levels. The results of this task are shown in Figure 7.2.

The first several times I read this research I was astounded. So much of what we teach is based on the assumption that children have already developed a strong understanding of place value by second grade, but, in fact, research shows that this is not so for many children. Many of the errors we see children make over and over again can be traced to a limited understanding or a misunderstanding of the base ten system.

From Research to Instruction: Problem-Solving with Ten in Grades One Through Three

Problem solving, with carefully chosen problem types and numbers, is one of the best ways to help children build strong understanding of the number system. In *Children's Mathematics,* Carpenter and his colleagues (1999) make a case for using certain types of multiplication and division problems with young children who are developing an understanding of base ten and place value. "When children have experiences with multiplication and division problems before they encounter base-ten concepts, they have the opportunity to develop an understanding of basic principles that are essential to understand base-ten numbers" (44). These particular problem types, described in Figure 7.3, are designed to encourage thinking about place value and constructing an understanding of how our number system works.

Figure 7.3 Multiplication and Division Problem Types That Build an Understanding of Place Value

Multiplication Grouping (No Extra)	Jackeline buys 4 boxes of oranges. There are 10 oranges in each box. How many oranges did Jackeline buy altogether?
Multiplication Grouping (Extra)	Ryan buys 3 boxes of oranges. There are 10 oranges in each box. He also buys a bag of 2 extra oranges. How many oranges did Ryan buy in all?
Measurement Division Note: *Measurement division* refers to problems in which the solver is looking for how many "containers" can be filled by a given number of objects. *Partitive division*, on the other hand, refers to problems in which the solver is looking for how many objects can be put in a given number of "containers."	Gabriela makes 27 cupcakes. She wants to put them in special boxes that hold 10 cupcakes. How many boxes can she fill? How many cupcakes will be left over?

Adapted from Carpenter et al. 1999, 45.

The Cupcake Problem in First Grade

Carlos and his dad bake _____ cupcakes for Carlos's birthday party. Carlos wants to put the cupcakes in special boxes that hold 10 cupcakes. How many boxes can he fill? How many extra cupcakes are left over?

This cupcake problem, along with the types of problems described in Figure 7.3, was designed to help children think about how our number system works and build a strong understanding of place value. In this particular problem, students are encouraged to think of groups of cupcakes both as ten individual cupcakes and one box of ten cupcakes. Both notions are held as equally true, just as the 2 in 24 is simultaneously two (groups of ten) and twenty.

During a math workshop in February, first-grade teacher Katie Keier and I sat down for some small-group math exchanges focusing on this cupcake problem. In order to collect a diverse range of strategies, we used 14 as the number of cupcakes for all of Katie's students, and then asked certain students to solve the problem again using the numbers 24 and 34 to see if their strategies would change and to see what kind of connections they would make between these numbers. As we watched these children problem solve, Katie and I had several questions in mind:

- How would students organize the fourteen cupcakes? What would this tell us about their understanding of the number ten?
- How would students explain their problem-solving process?
- Would children be able to unitize, or see the box of ten cupcakes as both one box of ten and ten individual cupcakes?

Mona's Strategies

Mona's process and strategies were particularly interesting. Before recording any ideas, Mona counted out fourteen Unifix cubes. She then separated ten cubes from her group of fourteen. Placing her hand over the group of ten and then pointing to the other four cubes, she said, "One box and four left over."

Mona's drawing of her idea (see Figure 7.4) was representative of a child beginning to unitize. She drew out fourteen cupcakes, starting a new row when dictated by the confines of the paper rather than numerically. She then recounted ten cupcakes and separated them with a line, labeling the cupcakes *1 Box* and *four left*. Interestingly, she added a picture of a large empty box for the ten cupcakes and a much smaller box for the "four left." She understood the difference in quantity between ten and four. She was also

Figure 7.4
Mona's Cupcake Problem

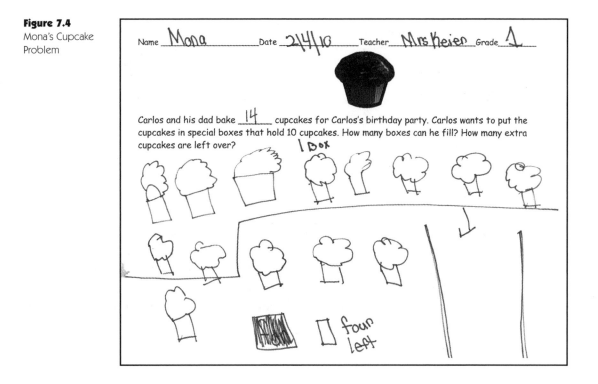

able to conceptualize the idea of the ten cupcakes as both ten individual cupcakes and one box.

Brian's Strategies

Brian represented his ideas on paper immediately, without using other tools. He drew a box and filled it with circles representing cupcakes, putting one cupcake outside the box. From listening to him retell the problem and explain his problem-solving process, it was clear he knew that there would be some leftover cupcakes that would not fit in the box, but he was not sure how many that would be. After recounting ten cupcakes, Brian put a box around the extras and wrote $4 + 10 = 14$ (see Figure 7.5).

Brian's drawing showed that he did not come into this problem knowing that fourteen was composed of ten and four. His organization was limited to the idea of "some in the box, some outside of the box." However, Brian built understanding through his problem solving when he was able to explain through his number sentence that four cupcakes and ten cupcakes made up the fourteen cupcakes that Carlos and his dad baked.

When Brian solved the same problem using 24 as the total number of cupcakes, he used a similar drawing strategy. Brian's picture clearly showed

Figure 7.5 Brian's Cupcake Problem with 14

Figure 7.6 Brian's Cupcake Problem with 24

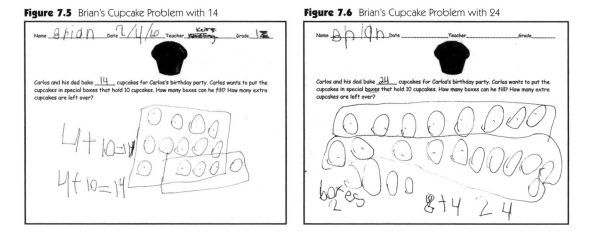

two groups of ten and four extras. He even wrote *boxes 2*. However, the number sentence he wrote was *2 + 4 24*. Unfortunately, I didn't see this part of his work at the time he was working on it. As his teacher, I might go back to him with the following questions:

- *I understand just what you did with your picture. Can you tell me more about the numbers you wrote here?*
- *I see the four extra cupcakes; where are the two that you wrote in your number sentence?*

Depending on Brian's responses, this might lead him to explain that the 2 in his work was two groups of ten, or twenty. However, it might reveal that Brian was not quite sure about the two boxes being simultaneously two boxes of ten and twenty individual cupcakes. Either way, it would help the teacher facilitate the math group and think about whose strategy Brian might listen to to help solidify his understanding.

David's Strategies

David struggled—in both literacy and math. He had to work really hard just to put together what was happening in the cupcake problem. I mention this not to emphasize David's struggles as a reader and mathematician, but to emphasize the strong thinking that is possible for all students when we give them the chance to try something challenging. What made David's strategy so interesting, and perhaps indicative of deeper understanding (or the ability to represent understanding) were his clear labels. He wrote *10* and *1* next to each other as he explained, "Ten cupcakes, one box" (see Figure 7.7). Although

Figure 7.7
David's Cupcake
Problem

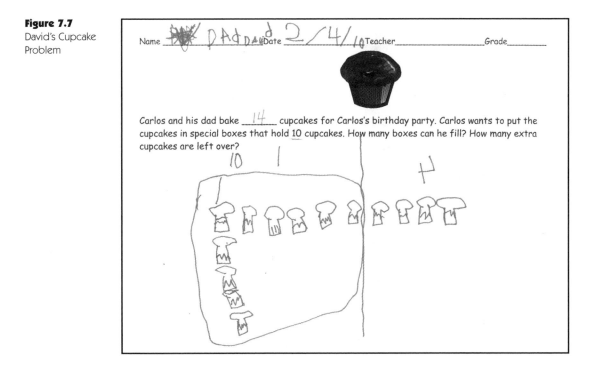

David's labeling might seem obvious to us as adults, the ability to see one group composed of ten objects both as one group and as ten objects is the very foundation on which an understanding of place value is built. In another classroom a teacher may have, with good intentions, decided that David needed more direct, explicit instruction—that he was the kind of student who needed this in order to master new ideas. In Katie's class David succeeded in spite of his struggles because he had a teacher who gave him repeated problem-solving experiences and guided his thinking throughout the math workshop (and especially in math exchanges), knowing that not all children come to the same understandings at the same time.

Alexandre's Strategies

Note: Although Alexandre transposed his numbers, writing *41* instead of *14*, he read his number sentences as "Fourteen minus ten is four."

Alexandre's strategy was similar to the preceding children's in that he started by drawing out the total number of cupcakes, fourteen, and then recounted and boxed ten of the cupcakes (see Figure 7.8). Unlike Brian, whose number sentence showed his understanding of the boxed cupcakes and the extras as part of the total number of cupcakes, Alexandre's number sentence,

Figure 7.8
Alexandre's
Cupcake Problem

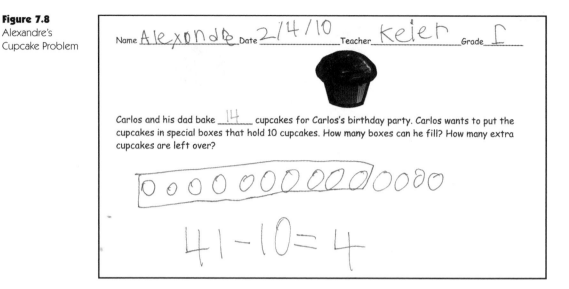

14 – 10 = 4, shows a slightly different, although equally valid, way of understanding the problem. When Alexandre talked about his work, he explained that the ten were being "taken away" from the rest of the cupcakes when they were put in the box, leaving the four extra cupcakes remaining. His number sentence matched his thought process.

Alexandre's process for solving the problem with twenty-four cupcakes was almost identical to that of his strategy when there were fourteen cupcakes. As his teacher, I might point to each digit in the number *24* and ask him, "Can you show me where this number is in the cupcakes you drew?" This would let me know whether he knew that the *2* in 24 cupcakes represented 20 or whether he still thought of 2 as only 2 cupcakes.

Suhani's Strategies

At first glance, Suhani's strategies looked very similar to those of the other children (see Figure 7.9). However, her work showed a deeper understanding of the ten-structure and base ten system. Unlike Alexandre, Brian, and Mona, who started by representing the total number of cupcakes, Suhani drew a box containing ten cupcakes and then counted on to fourteen while drawing the four remaining cupcakes. In her box of ten cupcakes, Suhani very deliberately illustrated the cupcakes in two rows of five. Katie and I wondered if this was just a coincidence or if it was evidence of deeper understanding. Here's how we followed up with questions about the cupcake problem:

Figure 7.9
Suhani's Cupcake
Problem with 14

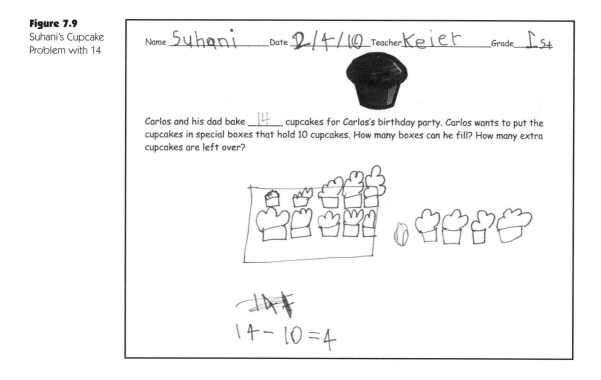

Katie: Guys, I'm noticing something different about how Suhani organizes the cupcakes in the box. Suhani, can you tell us about how you drew your ten cupcakes in the box? The rest of us are going to listen to see if we understand Suhani's ideas. (*Katie wanted to make sure she wasn't leading Suhani to an answer. She really wanted to know if this was a coincidence or if Suhani was using the five-structure to help her build the ten.*)

Suhani: Well, that was easy. One group of five and another group of five is ten.

Katie: Oh, so drawing the ten cupcakes in two groups of five helped you organize your ten cupcakes.

Suhani: Yeah, and now I can just see it's ten. (*Sweeping her finger across the groups of five cupcakes.*) Five and five make ten.

Mona: Yeah, then she knew she had exactly ten cause she could see real easy that she didn't leave any out or put too many in.

Later, when Katie asked Suhani to figure out how many boxes and extras Carlos would have if he wanted to make twenty-four cupcakes, she responded immediately. "Two boxes full of ten make twenty. Four extra is twenty-four." Only later did Suhani represent her ideas with drawings, keeping with the five-structure in her illustration of boxes of ten cupcakes (see Figure 7.10).

Figure 7.10
Suhani's Cupcake
Problem with 24

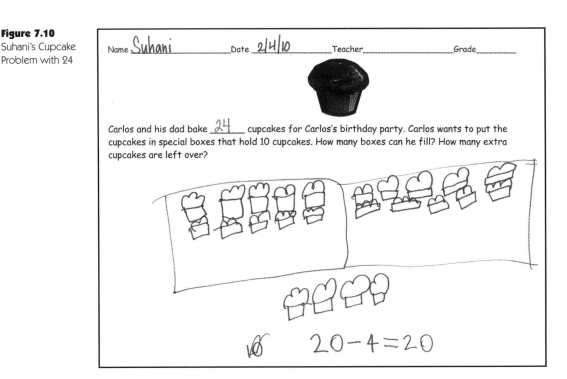

Suhani no longer needed the drawing model to solve the problem; however, she still held on to it, perhaps unsure how else to justify her answer. Though her number sentence *20 − 4 = 20* is incorrect, I believe this is more indicative of a child who is just beginning to connect her ideas and representations to standard notation, and not of her understanding of ten.

What Did These Children Have in Common?

All five of the students from Katie's first-grade class constructed models in order to solve problems. All of the students relied on tools or drawings to solve the cupcake problem. They followed the structure of the story problem. In fact, three of the students used fairly complex drawings of cupcakes instead of Brian's and Alexandre's more efficient representation of cupcakes as circles. Interestingly, one of Katie's students even mentioned, "I can use *x*'s to show the cupcakes," when thinking aloud about how she would solve the problem, yet when she actually began to draw her ideas, she drew cupcakes instead. Typical of students who model measurement division problems such as these, all of the first graders began by drawing the total number of cupcakes first and then separated the ten into a box. Even Suhani, who solved the problem of twenty-four cupcakes mentally first, still decided to model the problem by drawing all twenty-four cupcakes, divided into boxes and extras.

How Did These Children Differ in Understanding?

Unlike the other students in this diverse group, the fact that Suhani solved the problem of twenty-four cupcakes mentally indicated that she was already in the process of constructing an understanding of the base ten system and place value. Her understanding of our number system allowed her to mentally decompose the number 24 into 20 and 4 and understand that twenty-four is two groups of ten and four left over. The other first graders, on the other hand, relied on their drawings to solve this problem. They did not yet make a connection between the digit's place and its value. They did not yet fully understand 24 as the same as 20 and 4. They were on their way though, and with more problems like the cupcake one they would begin to see a connection.

It was a great moment when later in the year a first grader working on a problem about packaging strawberries into packs of ten (a problem designed to encourage an understanding of place value and the number system) announced, "Hey! I see something important. When there were 53 strawberries that was 5 packs of 10 and 3 extras. When there were 37 strawberries that was 3 packs of 10 and 7 extras. It's a pattern. You don't have to draw it every time. So, for 29 strawberries that's like 20 plus 9 so 2 packs and 9 extras." This deep understanding of how numbers are composed and decomposed and the ability to see the *2* in 29 as simultaneously 2 packs of 10 strawberries and 20 strawberries takes time to develop in the mind of the child. But it is worth every moment! Unlike the child who has "learned place value" procedurally through a rote memorization of tens and ones, this child working on the strawberry problems understood how numbers work and would take this understanding with him as he encountered more complex problems and larger numbers.

How Can a Teacher Help Children Like These Learn from One Another?

The role of the teacher in math exchanges is to facilitate and mediate children's thinking. This is best accomplished by asking specific questions and having a particular reason in mind when choosing students to share their problem-solving strategies. Children listen to the strategies of others and respond with their own thinking. These are some questions that would facilitate thinking for mathematicians similar to those in Katie's first-grade class:

• *So when there were fourteen cupcakes you each drew ten cupcakes in the box. How did you figure out how many extras there were?* (Possible responses may include using drawing to model the problem without a lot of strategic thinking about the number, counting on from ten, using a known fact such as 10 + 4 or 14 − 4, or noticing 4 in the ones place. You can highlight certain strategies by asking a student with more efficient strategies—like Suhani—to share with the group and then asking, "Did anyone see how Suhani figured this out? How did she know there would be four extra cupcakes even before she did her drawing?")

- *What do you notice about how Suhani organized her cupcakes? Did she do anything different?* (This allows the teacher to highlight Suhani's more efficient structure, lets Suhani clarify why she did what she did, and allows other students time to study Suhani's work.)

- *What if Carlos and his dad make fifty-seven cupcakes? How many boxes do you think that they would fill?* (This allows the teacher to see what mental strategies students can extend, and if their ideas are reasonable.)

Where Should These Children Go Next?

Many first-grade students are still in the emergent phases of building number sense that includes a deep understanding of ten. For these children, having many experiences to participate in math exchanges with story problems and routines (explained later in this chapter) that encourage thinking about ten and groups of ten is important. Children need time to explore these ideas and they often develop this understanding at different rates. You may find investigations that are appropriate for your whole class or for small groups in your own textbook or in other resources available at your school. Additional resources are suggested in Figure 7.11.

For students like Suhani who have developed some understanding of the base ten system and place value, teachers can encourage students to move toward more efficient strategies and representations by increasing the number. If the number is high enough, students may decide that it is not worth their time to draw or model out each individual item. Students like

Figure 7.11 Instructional Resources for Building an Understanding of Ten

Constance Kamii, *Young Children Reinvent Arithmetic: Implications of Piaget's Theory*, 2nd edition, 2000

Kathy Richardson, *Developing Number Concepts, Book 3: Place Value, Multiplication, and Division*, 1998

John Van de Walle and LouAnn Lovin, *Teaching Student-Centered Mathematics: Grades K–3*, 2006

Maryann Wickett and Marilyn Burns, *Teaching Arithmetic: Lessons for Introducing Place Value, Grade 2*, 2002

Maryann Wickett and Marilyn Burns, *Teaching Arithmetic: Lessons for Extending Place Value, Grade 3*, 2005

Suhani should be encouraged to express that twenty-four is composed of (and can be decomposed into) a group of twenty (or two groups of ten) and four ones or extras.

Try It Out!
The Bakery Project

Let students know that they will be working in a bakery and filling cupcake orders for different customers. Give different numbers to different children (14, 29, 32, 57, 108). Remind them that in this bakery, ten cupcakes fit in each box. If there are extra cupcakes that won't fill a box, these cupcakes are wrapped and packaged individually. Have each child make a small poster showing how he or she packaged each bakery order. Children should have access to paper, pens, and empty ten-frames (if you use these in your class and children are familiar with them). Observe how students solve the problem with these numbers:

- Do students become more efficient in their strategies with larger numbers, or do they still need more time to explore and construct understanding with modeling?
- Do students make a connection between the number of boxes and the number of extras and the total number of cupcakes? For example, here's what you might say to a child who has just finished solving the cupcake problem with the number 32:

Teacher: So, how many cupcakes did Carlos and his dad bake?
Child: Thirty-two.
Teacher: Yes, you wrote that number right in the problem. So, (*pointing to the digit 2 in 32*), where is this part in your work?
Child: The two extra cupcakes.
Teacher: (*Pointing at the digit 3*) And, what about this part? Where is that in your work?

Possible Child Responses Indicating Level of Understanding
1. The child is unsure or does not provide a response.
2. Child identifies three individual cupcakes.
3. "The three is three groups [boxes] of ten." Or "The three means thirty."

❖❖❖

The in-depth analysis of first graders solving the cupcake problem illustrates how much teacher knowledge can be gained through a few short math exchanges with students, and how this knowledge can help the teacher guide the next steps for individual students, groups of students, and the class as a whole.

The Cupcake Problem in Second Grade

Walking into second-year teacher Rachel Knieling's second-grade math workshop is like a breath of fresh mathematical air. Every student is purposefully engaged. As Rachel finishes her focus lesson, children quickly find their math partners and sit down to play a game Rachel has purposely selected, taught, and reflected on with the children.

One day Rachel and I sat down with a group of five students. "Are you here to talk about brownies?" Angel asked me. He remembered that the last time I visited we worked on sharing two brownies with three friends. Angel really gets into the contexts of the problems he solves with his math partner. And, like me, he enjoys working on problems related to food!

"Today I've brought a problem about my friend Anthony, who is bringing cupcakes to school to share with his friends on his birthday," I responded. (In her first-grade class, Katie Keier had used the name Carlos in the cupcake problem because she had a student by that name.)

"Oh, yeah, Jhenny brought cupcakes on her birthday—the chocolate kind with white stuff on top."

"Icing," said Jhenny, Angel's partner. "I brought one for everyone in the class and one for Ms. Knieling too."

After a few moments of discussion of our favorite kinds of cupcakes and on which special occasions we eat cupcakes, Rachel and I introduced the story problem in much the same way Katie introduced the problem to her first-grade students. We made sure to check for understanding of the problem, asking students to retell it.

After students retold the problem, I asked them to write in the number 34 as the number of cupcakes in the story. I thought 34 would be a number all of the second graders would be comfortable with and a number that would allow different strategies and understandings to be illuminated.

As when I worked with Katie's class, Rachel and I had a lot of questions in mind about how students would solve this problem:

- Would most second graders still draw the individual cupcakes in each box?
- How would students organize the groups of cupcakes?

- What sense would the students make about the connection between the number of boxes of cupcakes, the extra cupcakes, and the total number of cupcakes?
- Would they wonder why thirty-four cupcakes resulted in three boxes and four extras, or would they see this as a happy coincidence?
- Would students change their strategies as the numbers got bigger?

As a math teacher, I'm always on the edge of my seat as I watch students thinking and constructing meaning from a story problem!

Lucy's Strategies

Of all the students whom I watched solve this problem, Lucy was the most fascinating to me. As I watched Lucy solve the thirty-four-cupcake problem, she struggled to draw boxes of ten cupcakes while simultaneously keeping track of the total number of cupcakes. Once she realized she had too many cupcakes in a box, she would return to cross some out and begin counting again (see Figure 7.12). Her boxes of ten showed that she did not yet know how to organize a group of objects in an effective way (such as using two rows of five to make ten). Lucy's counting and recounting as she juggled keeping track of putting ten cupcakes in a box and drawing a total of thirty-four

Figure 7.12

Lucy's Cupcake Problem with 34

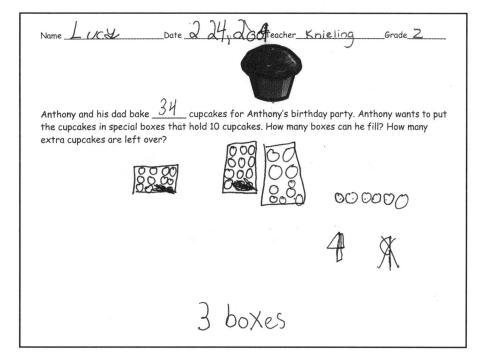

cupcakes resulted in miscounting. She drew six extra cupcakes rather than four although she did record the number *4* after listening to another child explain his strategy.

Lucy, a quiet English language learner, rarely shared her own strategies. While discussing the initial cupcake problem with the number 34, I asked students who had more efficient counting strategies to share why they chose their strategies over drawing all thirty-four cupcakes.

Rachel and I were not sure if Lucy understood when her classmates explained their more efficient strategies or if she needed more experiences to clarify the understanding of ten cupcakes as both individual cupcakes and as one box.

After quickly looking at our list of possible numbers for this problem, Rachel and I chose to try the problem again with seventy-four cupcakes. In some cases, using larger numbers can actually promote more efficient strategies; children no longer want to draw seventy-four individual cupcakes and begin thinking about how to use more efficient notation and strategies.

Rachel and I were delighted to see Lucy's work with seventy-four cupcakes (see Figure 7.13). She began the problem similarly, by drawing a box and drawing a cupcake inside. Then, pausing, and looking around at how others in her group were solving, she wrote the number *10* above the box and continued drawing boxes and labeling the tens while whisper-counting by tens to herself. Last, she drew the four extra cupcakes, and wrote *7 boxes* and *4 out*. Amazing! Lucy understood the inefficiency of drawing all the cupcakes and was able to construct the groups of ten numerically through a counting strategy rather than by direct modeling.

Figure 7.13
Lucy's Cupcake
Problem with 74

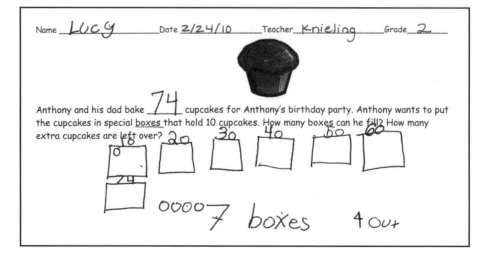

Not wanting to miss an opportunity to reinforce Lucy's leap in thinking and representation, Rachel asked, "Lucy, you really changed your strategy. Tell us how you changed your ideas."

Quietly, Lucy replied, "Counting by tens is faster. I know to stop at 70 because it's just 71, 72, 73, 74."

"Oh," said Rachel. "There aren't enough cupcakes to make another group of ten." Rachel turned to the rest of the group. "It looks like Lucy changed some of her ideas and used a more efficient strategy. Did any of you find a more efficient strategy to use the second time we solved this problem?"

When Rachel and I reflected on Lucy's thinking after school, we agreed that although Lucy's go-to strategy was drawing individual cupcakes in boxes, she was already in the process of constructing the idea of ten as ten ones and one group of ten.

Lucy hovered between more and less efficient modeling and counting strategies to solve the cupcake problems. Her change in strategies may not have been a permanent one at this point, but it did give Rachel an idea of how to help Lucy move along in her understanding.

Jeffrey's Strategies

Jeffrey emerged as one of the stronger students in his understanding of the cupcake problem when solving with the number 34. In fact, it was he who explained to Lucy, "You don't need to draw out all the cupcakes because one box is ten, two boxes is twenty, three boxes is thirty, and then four more."

As we thought about where to go next with Jeffrey, I asked Rachel, "What do you think he'll do with a number greater than 100?"

"I'm not sure," she replied. "Let's try it out."

Jeffrey initially was not intimidated by the 134-cupcake problem. He quickly wrote the number *10* repeatedly to count up to 100 (see Figure 7.14). (Note: Jeffrey actually wrote *10* only nine times; however, he double-counted one *10* and thus believed he had reached a total of 100.)

What was most interesting about Jeffrey was that although he understood the idea of groups of ten up to 100, he did not extend this knowledge past 100, as he wrote the numerals *101* through *134*.

When I asked Jeffrey how many boxes he filled and how many extra cupcakes he had, he looked at his work, confused. He knew something was not quite right, but he was not sure what it was.

Many of us have had the experience of listening to young children count by tens. I always listen anxiously as they approach 100. What will they say next? It is not uncommon to hear children count ". . . 80, 90, 100, 200" or

Figure 7.14

Jeffrey's Cupcake
Problem with 134

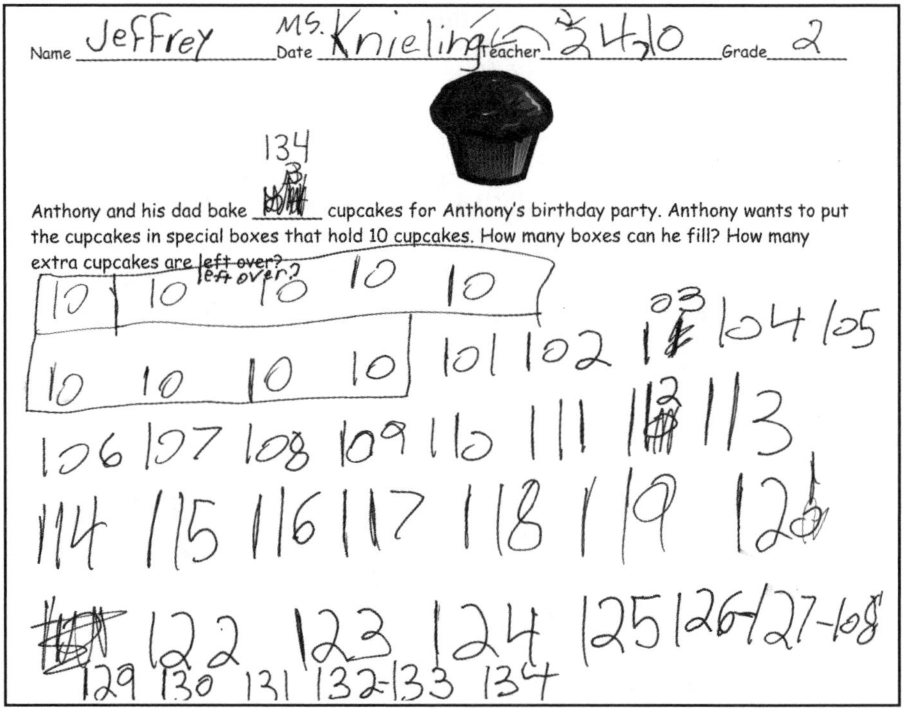

"...80, 90, 100, 101" or "...80, 90, 100, 1,000," or for children simply to stop at 100 as if there were no further numbers when counting by tens.

Rachel's observation of Jeffrey's work led her to believe that Jeffrey needed more experiences extending his place-value understanding and knowledge about numbers past 100.

Sandra's and Luke's Strategies

All of the second graders described so far drew in order to solve the problem. Although Sandra also relied on her drawing to solve the problems, her work with seventy-four cupcakes showed that she was beginning to understand the system behind the problem (see Figure 7.15). After completing her drawing and writing *7 boxes full* and *4 left*, Sandra decomposed the number 74, showing that *70* and *7* belonged to her drawing of 70 cupcakes and that the *4* in 74 belonged to the "4 left." While Sandra was moving toward fully understanding the base ten system (within ones, tens, and hundreds), Luke, on the other hand, solved the problems mentally.

When solving the cupcake problem with 134 cupcakes, Luke immediately wrote, *He can fill 13 boxes. There are 4 cupcakes left over.* (See Figure 7.16.) Rachel prompted Luke to explain his thinking, something he was often

Figure 7.15

Sandra's Cupcake Problem with 74

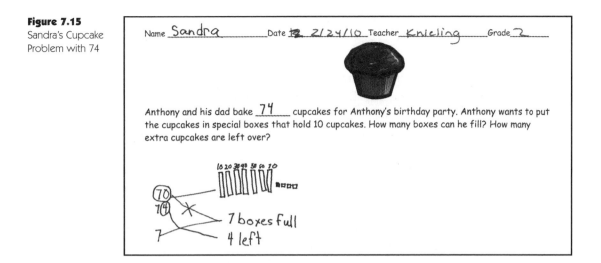

resistant to do. In fact, Luke sometimes struggled to explain exactly how he knew what he knew, so Rachel had been focusing on getting him to slow down and think about his problem-solving process. After thinking for a while, Luke wrote, *He can fill 13 because there are ten ten's in a hundred and 3 in 30, so 10 + 3 = 13.* Clearly Luke could simultaneously think of individual cupcakes and groups of ten cupcakes. When he wrote *10 + 3 = 13,* he knew

Figure 7.16

Luke's Cupcake Problem with 134

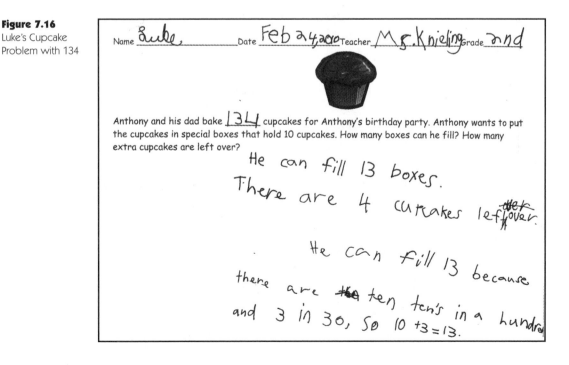

the numerals were referring to 10 groups of ten and 3 groups of ten and were equal to 13 groups of ten.

What Did These Children Have in Common?

Sandra, Jeffrey, and Lucy (in her second problem) all used a skip-counting strategy. They also all still needed to draw something representing the "box of ten" so that they could later go back and count the groups of tens by ones to determine how many boxes there were.

Where Did They Differ in Their Understanding?

Jeffrey and Luke showed slightly different thinking when there were 134 cupcakes. Jeffrey had not extended his thinking of tens past 100, as evidenced by the fact that he counted by ones from 101 to 134, and was not sure how to answer the questions, "How many boxes can he fill?" and "How many extra cupcakes are left over?"

Luke, on the other hand, had the flexibility to understand that 134 is simultaneously 1 hundred, 3 tens, and 4 ones as well as 10 tens, 3 tens, and 4 ones, as he explained on his paper. Luke's flexible thinking served him well in computation with the ability to decompose numbers in different ways to solve problems efficiently.

How Can a Teacher Help Children Like These Learn from One Another?

Lucy and Sandra will benefit from many of the teacher moves described as appropriate for Katie's first graders. However, they are ready to start thinking about three-digit numbers and how they fit into our base-ten system.

Where Should These Children Go Next?

Many of the routines and problem-solving situations described in this chapter are appropriate for this second-grade group of children. However, for Luke, who is more advanced in his understanding of base ten and place value, I might extend the cupcake problem with the following problem:

> Anthony and Fatima bake cupcakes together for a big party. They make 134 chocolate cupcakes and 257 vanilla cupcakes. Both Anthony and Fatima put the cupcakes in special boxes that hold 10 cupcakes. How many boxes can they fill? How many extra cupcakes are left over?

Would Luke use what he already knows about 134 to solve this problem or would he start over? How would he decompose the numbers? Would he decompose 257 into 2 hundreds, 5 tens, and 7 ones, or into 25 tens and 7 ones? How would he combine the chocolate and vanilla cupcakes? If Luke solved this problem using the traditional algorithm, would he be able to explain and bring meaning to the procedure? This problem would be certain to push Luke's understanding of the number system and increase his flexibility as he explained his thinking and shared strategies with others.

The Cupcake Problem in Third Grade

The development of mathematical thinking is not linear. Some older students unfamiliar with problem solving or with a particular problem type will use modeling strategies very similar to those of students in first grade. Even with solid instruction, children develop understanding and efficient strategies for problem solving at different rates. The following are some examples of the cupcake problem from students in Phoebe Markle's third-grade class and students from my own third-grade class.

Cristian's Strategies

Cristian's work, like that of other students who have not constructed the idea of ten as simultaneously ten ones and one ten, showed confusion in keeping track of how many cupcakes to place in a box while also keeping track of the total number of cupcakes. His work showed no strategic organization of the ten cupcakes (see Figure 7.17). Despite the fact that Cristian was a third grader, he had not yet fully developed an understanding of the base ten system. Later, after listening to other children in his group explain their strategies, Cristian was able to articulate why some children drew boxes with the number 10 inside rather than drawing ten individual cupcakes. When solving the cupcake problem with 74, Cristian was able to apply this strategy to his

Figure 7.17
Cristian's Cupcake
Problem with 14

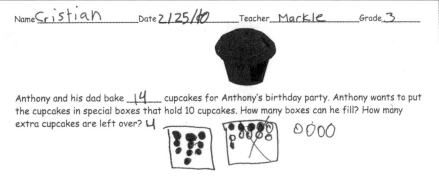

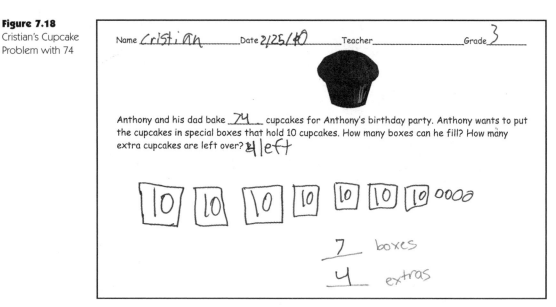

own work (see Figure 7.18). Still, like second grader Lucy, Cristian will need many more opportunities to construct deep understanding of base ten before his more efficient strategies for problem solving move from mimicking to true understanding.

Many other third-grade students used strategies similar to Cristian's as well as those of Rachel's second graders and Katie's first graders. As Kamii's (1994, 2000) and Ross's (1986, 1990) research showed, even as our curriculum demands that children extend understanding and computation to larger and larger numbers in third grade, we must continue to give them opportunities to frame their work within a strong understanding of base ten.

Michael's Strategy

Michael's strategy was a good example of how students move away from modeling and counting strategies when deep understanding of base ten is present. Michael had extended his understanding of the base ten system into the hundreds. He decomposed the number 134 by circling the 13, indicating he understood that 13 tens is equal to 130 and that there were 4 cupcakes left over (see Figure 7.19). A child with less understanding of place value and base ten might have needed to see the 1 digit as 100 and the 3 digit as 30 and decomposed these numbers separately. Michael had the flexibility to choose the most efficient strategy for what he was trying to figure out—how many boxes of ten cupcakes Anthony can fill.

Figure 7.19

Michael's Cupcake
Problem with 134

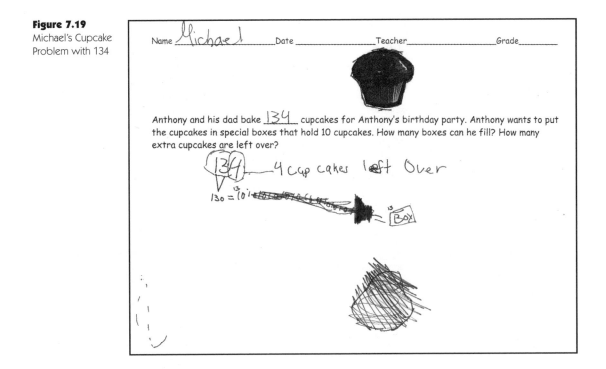

Math Club—Continuing to Build
True Understanding of Ten

One of the most interesting insights I have had about children's developing understanding of the concept of ten was with a group of second graders who came to a math club before school every day for six weeks. Although all of these students were chosen by their teachers as students who "struggled with number sense," their diverse thinking and abilities provided a rich environment for exploring the importance of ten.

"We've been doing a lot of counting by tens lately," I commented to the group about a week into our sessions. "I'm wondering if we always have to start at 10 when we count by tens. Could we start at 14 or 7 or 105?"

"No!" the group said, almost in chorus.

Anthony confidently added, "You could start at ten or zero or fifty, but not at those other numbers. Those aren't ten numbers."

"What are ten numbers?" I asked the group.

"You know," Ohmad replied. "Ten, 20, 30, 40, 50, 60, on and on to infinity."

"So, what makes these numbers ten numbers?" I asked.

"They all have a zero," Khadija commented.

"A zero," I repeated. "Do you all understand what Khadija is telling us?"

"Yes, yes. There's a zero in the ones place," said Victory. "See?" she said, pointing to a hundreds chart. "Zero in the ones place and then 1, 2, 3, 4, 5, 6, up and up and up in the tens place."

I was startled by what I was hearing. I knew these second graders had had experience counting by tens starting at nondecade numbers in their classrooms. I knew they solved problems using base ten blocks. And yet, to this group of children, the importance and usefulness of ten was a concept that had not yet been fully explored or accepted.

Later that afternoon, after the children had all left for the day, I sat down to reflect on this group of second-grade mathematicians. As I looked through their initial interview preassessments and the story problems we had been working on, I realized that I should not have been at all shocked that this group of children believed that counting by tens starting from a nondecade number was impossible. Figure 7.20 shows some of the strategies that I saw in their initial work. You will probably recognize a few from your own students, as many of them are common strategies used by children who don't have a basic understanding of the base ten system. When I reflect on my students' work, I often use the table format in Figure 7.20 to help me delve into their understanding and misconceptions.

So, what should our students understand about base ten and place value throughout their elementary school years? What are the big ideas they must construct in order to have a deep understanding of base ten and place value? Van de Walle and Lovin (2006) write:

> In grades K and 1 children count and are exposed to patterns in numbers to 100. Most importantly, they begin to think about groups of ten as a unit. By second grade, these initial ideas of patterns and groups of ten are formally connected to our place-value system of numeration. This is no small achievement! Ample time should be given to this development. In grade 3 the system is expanded into three or four digits. (122)

Although Van de Walle and Lovin describe skills and understandings by grade level, it is important to note that these understandings often cross grade-level boundaries, as we have seen throughout this chapter.

While there are many models and tools that support children's understanding of the base ten number system, it is important not to confuse the

Figure 7.20 Second Graders' Preassessment Problem-Solving Strategies

Story Problem (Join Result Unknown):

Marvin loves to read. On Saturday he read 22 pages. On Sunday he read 10 more pages. How many pages did Marvin read this weekend?

Student Work/ Strategies/Tools Used	What Does the Student Know?	What Does the Student Almost Know?	Next Steps
Strategy 1 (used by 2 of 8 students) Student counts out 22 cubes in one pile and counts out 10 cubes in another pile. Student recounts starting at 1. (I refer to this strategy as *counting three times*, because the student counts each group and then counts a third time when joining them together.)	Student understands that this problem involves putting two parts together to make a whole, and thus adds the numbers together.	Depending on the student, given smaller numbers the student may have *counted on* (started with one number in his or her head and used some kind of tool to count on the second number).	• Counting on • Noticing patterns when 10 is added to another number • Practicing counting by tens starting at decade and nondecade numbers • Noticing what changes and what stays the same with the numbers when counting by tens
Strategy 2 (used by 3 of 8 students) Student holds 22 in his or her mind and uses fingers, cubes, base ten blocks, hundreds chart, or writing/drawing to count on 10 more.	In addition to the preceding understanding: • Student understands how to count on.	• Student may have experience counting by tens. • Student may be able to recognize patterns when making jumps of ten while counting. (I.e., the ones number never changes; the tens number goes up by one number each time.)	• Noticing patterns when 10 is added to another number • Practicing counting by tens starting at decade and nondecade numbers • Noticing what changes and what stays the same with the numbers when counting by tens • Beginning to make jumps of ten with tools (see Strategy 3)
Strategy 3 (used by 2 of 8 students) Student makes a jump of ten from 22 on the number grid (one box down), open number line, or other tool, rather than counting on one by one.	In addition to the preceding understandings: • Student understands that making jumps of ten is more efficient than counting on one by one.	• Student may have an understanding of ten and how numbers change when making jumps of ten.	• Noticing patterns when 10 is added to another number • Practicing counting by tens starting at decade and nondecade numbers • Noticing what changes and what stays the same with the numbers when counting by tens • Without tools, beginning to make jumps of ten from comfortable numbers (see Strategy 4)
Strategy 4 (used by 1 of 8 students) Student automatically says, "Thirty-two," and can explain something like, "Twenty-two and 10 more is 32."	In addition to the preceding understandings: • Student understands how numbers change as he or she makes jumps of ten and ten. • Student understands ten as a special or important number.	• Student may understand how to make combinations of jumps of ten and one, changing from counting by tens to counting by ones.	• Noticing patterns when 10 is added to another number • Practicing counting by tens starting at two- and three-digit decade and nondecade numbers • Noticing what changes and what stays the same with the numbers when counting by tens • Practicing counting by hundreds and comparing and contrasting counting by tens and hundreds • Problem solving that involves a jump of ten and multiples of ten from a three-digit decade or nondecade number (e.g., 250 + 10 or 164 + 30)

ability to manipulate tools and construct models with deep understanding of the base ten system. For example, Van de Walle and Lovin point out that "with minimal instruction children can tell you that in the numeral 53, the 5 is in the tens place or that there are '3 ones.' However, it is likely that this is simply a naming of positions with little understanding . . . It is easy to attach words to both materials and groups without realizing what the materials or symbols represent" (2006, 124).

Indeed, I saw this firsthand with the second graders with whom I was working. During the first couple of days of the math club, I interviewed each child to get to know them as mathematicians and to collect some initial data.

As you can see in Figures 7.21 and 7.22, most students were successful both in recognizing and in building quantities using base ten blocks. However, their use and understanding of the manipulatives did not necessarily indicate deep understanding of base ten or correspond to the strategies they used during problem solving. Many of the children who easily completed the tasks in Figures 7.21 and 7.22 did not demonstrate understanding of the base ten number system when problem solving. Most students relied on inefficient modeling and counting strategies; they did not employ any strategic use of ten. While I believe the questions on the interview assessment (Figures 7.21 and 7.22) did provide some useful information, it is important to remember that they provide only part of the big picture of the child's understanding.

Reflecting on the children's comments about counting, their interview assessment data, and the strategies they used during our initial math exchanges together, I chose to focus our math club time on developing a deep understanding of base ten. Did these children struggle with other

Figure 7.21 Second Graders' Responses to Preassessment Interview Question 3

Question 3:					
Teacher puts out 2 tens blocks and 3 ones cubes and asks, "What number is this?" **Objective:** Recognizing an amount in tens and ones; counting by tens; counting up; base ten/place-value understanding	Is familiar with base ten blocks	Counts by tens to 20 and then counts on by ones	Counts on from 20	Has a strategy for keeping track of base ten blocks (e.g., counts with eyes, counts by touch, etc.)	The strategy works (student solves correctly)
Total Number of Students: 8	8 of 8 students	8 of 8 students	0 of 8 students	8 of 8 students	7 of 8 students Incorrect response: 32

Figure 7.22 Second Graders' Responses to Preassessment Interview Question 4

Question 4:	Uses 1 ten block and 7 ones cubes	Uses 17 ones cubes	Counts on from 17 • in head • with blocks or fingers	Recounts beginning at 1 (or 10) and counts all
"Show me 17 with ten blocks and ones cubes." After child has built 17 the teacher adds 3 more ones cubes to the pile, and asks, "How many now?" **Objective:** Building amount using base ten blocks; counting on; base-ten/place-value sense				
Total Number of Students: 8	4 of 8 students Unable to respond: 1 of 8 students Builds 70 instead of 17: 1 of 8 students	2 of 8 students	In head: 2 of 8 students With blocks or fingers: 4 of 8 students	0 of 8 students

mathematical concepts? Certainly. However, I knew I needed to make instructional decisions that were most responsive to their learning needs. While the grade-level expectation for second grade meant that these children were learning to add and subtract two-digit numbers in their classrooms, I did not believe this was the most responsive or responsible decision for the children I was working with in math club. Unless this group of children developed a strong understanding of base ten, they would continue to use inefficient counting-on strategies or adding and subtracting tens and ones with only superficial understanding of what they were doing, and would thus become less and less accurate with their calculations as they continued to work with larger numbers.

How We Constructed an Understanding of Base Ten

Constructing a deep and true understanding of the base ten number system does not occur overnight. Neither is there such a thing as a "quick fix" for students struggling with number sense related to an understanding of how numbers work. True understanding is built over time as a result of many opportunities to investigate how numbers work. These are some of the repeated experiences I used with the second-grade math club to help them construct this understanding.

Daily Routines

Counting Around the Circle

We focused on counting by tens starting at nondecade numbers and counting past 100. Children said the numbers, while I recorded them in a way that drew attention to the patterns occurring. We then discussed the number patterns we discovered and recorded our ideas. Every day we counted, we checked our recorded ideas about counting (or making jumps of ten) to make sure our ideas were "always true."

We also counted by twos, fives, hundreds, and thousands, starting from zero and from other numbers and noticing the patterns.

Dot Cards and Ten-Frames

We also periodically (about two times a week for five minutes each session) used dot cards and ten-frames to help children strengthen their ability to subitize and see ten as a unit composed of various parts.

Counting Collections

For this routine, I provided a countable collection and asked, "How could we count the _____?" I accepted all answers. Then, kids tried out the strategies and discussed efficient ways of grouping. Even older children benefit from working on counting collections!

Fish in the Bucket Game: First Few Times We Played

In this game I put a certain number of Unifix cubes (or other uniform objects, such as hexagon pattern blocks or color tiles) in a bucket. The first few times we played the game I asked for suggestions of how we could organize the "fish" so they would be easy to keep track of and count. Sometimes during these first few sessions students made one long train of the objects or grouped the objects by twos, fives, or tens.

Fish in the Bucket Game: Subsequent Games

Here's how we played the game after children had generally agreed that ten was a useful number for organizing and counting:

Teacher: Look at the fish I caught in my bucket! How many groups of ten fish do you think are in my bucket?

We recorded estimates. Then students went to work organizing the "fish" into groups of ten and extra fish.

Teacher: So, how many fish were in my bucket? How did you make groups to help yourself figure it out?

Children explained their various counting methods. In a recent game with forty-three fish, I heard the following different ways of counting. Figure 7.23 shows how these students initially counted the groups they had built.

Eric: Ten, 20, 30, 40, 50, 60, 70. There are 70 fish.
Luz: One, 2, 3, 4, 5, 6, 7. There are 7 groups.
Jennifer: Ten, 20, 30, 40, 41, 42, 43. There are 43 fish. Four groups of 10 fish and 3 extras.

Eric's and Luz's errors are some of the most common errors that occur in this kind of task when children are still in the process of developing understanding of the system of tens. As they struggle to maintain the concept of ten being simultaneously one group of tens and ten groups of one, they easily confuse whether and when to count by tens or ones. The beauty of this small-group experience was that I didn't need to show Eric and Luz how to "correctly" count the fish and tell how many groups there were.

Teacher: Hmm . . . We have some different ideas. I wrote all of your ideas on the board. What do you all think?
Eric: Oh, yeah, I need to count again.

Figure 7.23 Students' Counting of Fish in a Bucket

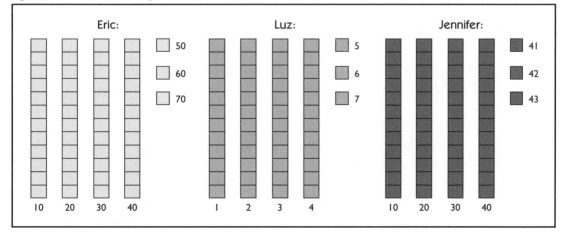

When recounting, Eric made the switch between groups of tens and ones. This didn't mean that Eric wouldn't make this same error again. However, the more experiences he had to build his understanding of the base ten system, the stronger he would become with this game and, more important, his understanding of the number system.

After children played this game a few more times, I introduced a chart on which we recorded the number of groups of fish, the number of extra fish, and the total number of fish. This launched us into a discussion of what patterns we saw and why these patterns were occurring.

Problem-Solving Math Exchanges

Each day in math club we gathered as a group to read and retell a story problem that focused on some aspect of building understanding of base ten. Children solved problems independently, and then we debriefed as a group. Some of our problems were based on the types of multiplication and division problems referred to in Figure 7.3. The following are some examples of additional problem types we used; the types are based on the work of Carpenter and his colleagues (1999).

Join Result Unknown

Ohmad is collecting aluminum cans for the Recycling Club. He collects _____ cans from Ms. Wedekind's classroom and _____ cans from Ms. Keier's classroom. How many cans does Ohmad collect for the Recycling Club?

Separate Result Unknown

Some second graders are observing crickets outside. They see _____ crickets in the grass. Then _____ crickets hop away. How many crickets are in the grass now?

Part-Part-Whole, Part Unknown

Khadija and Marvin are helping to sharpen a lot of pencils in their classroom. Khadija sharpened _____ pencils. Marvin sharpened some pencils. Together they sharpened _____ pencils. How many pencils did Marvin sharpen?

Compare Difference Unknown

(Note: These types of problems are usually some of the most difficult for children to solve because of the lack of action in the problem. See the problem variation as a scaffold that may be helpful for your students.)

Hector has _____ goldfish crackers for snack. Jackeline has _____ goldfish crackers. How many more goldfish crackers does Hector have than Jackeline?

Variation:

Hector has _____ goldfish crackers for snack. Jackeline has _____ goldfish crackers for snack. Who has more crackers? How many more goldfish crackers does Jackeline need to take from the box of crackers to have the same number as Hector?

Number Suggestions for the Preceding Problems

- Focusing on jumps of ten from decade numbers: 40, 50; 30, 50; 80, 100; 80, 110
- Focusing on a single jump of ten from nondecade numbers: 36, 10; 13, 10; 124, 10; 104, 10
- Focusing on multiple jumps of ten from nondecade numbers: 56, 20; 78, 30; 124, 20; 104, 20; 204, 20
- Focusing on decomposing numbers for computational efficiency: 44, 12; 50, 12; 75, 27

As the math club was winding up for the year, I gave this problem to Brandon:

54 fish swim by in the stream. The hungry brown bear scoops up 15 fish and eats them. How many fish keep swimming down the stream?

"Let's see," considered Brandon. "Fifty-four minus 10 is 44. When you count by tens the ones don't change. Then 44 minus 4 is 40 and minus 1 more is 39."

To solve problems similar to this one earlier in the year, Brandon's strategy had been to use a hundreds chart to count backward by ones. He was all "grab and compute" and no strategy. His experiences with grouping problems, such as those in the fish-in-a-bucket routine, and looking for patterns while skip-counting helped move Brandon's understanding along. He showed a lot in this one exchange—an understanding of how numbers change with jumps of ten, how to split numbers for more efficient computation, and how to decompose five to make solving 44 – 5 easier.

Some children need more time and more problem-solving experiences than other children to deeply understand. I cannot say that the children in math club never again struggled with mathematical understanding. Not all children changed in the profound ways that Brandon did. However, many of the children in this group did leave with a more solidly constructed understanding of how numbers work, and as a result, more effective and efficient strategies for computation.

8

Reflection and Self-Monitoring

ONE OF MY GREATEST HOPES is for my students to become empowered learners. I think of an empowered mathematical learner as a child who does the following:

- Takes ownership of her learning
- Believes he is the kind of person who works hard and takes on challenges
- Self-monitors for changes in her own thinking and strategies
- Sees confusion, difficulty, and wrong answers not as signs of failure, but as part of the journey toward becoming a stronger, wiser mathematician
- Self-advocates for himself as a learner, actively questioning and seeking clarification and meaning from others as well as from himself

We, as teachers, can and should strive to teach children to become empowered learners. Teaching children to be reflective learners is the first step in this direction.

Reflection in the Math Exchange: Slowing Down Thinking to Go Deep

As you'll recall from Chapter 1, reflection is how we end each daily math workshop at Bailey's Elementary School. However, I believe that becoming a reflective learner begins long before the last five or ten minutes of math workshop.

In order to help children become reflective learners we first need to model and tell stories about our own thinking and our own reflective practices and ask children to do the same. One way to do this is through the mathematician statements discussed throughout this book. When beginning a math exchange I often remind students of a mathematician statement we have previously discussed that relates to the goals or purpose of our meeting.

One day in November I was teaching a small group of first graders. "Remember," I told them as we sat down in a circle on the floor to begin the math exchange, "mathematicians look for many ways to take numbers apart and put them together. In this problem I want to see how you can do this." I went on to tell a story problem to the four kids seated with me.

"Last night I decided to bake some cupcakes for my book club. I knew ten people would be at the book club meeting including myself, and I decided to bake chocolate and lemon cupcakes. If everyone ate one cupcake, what different combinations of chocolate and lemon cupcakes could have been eaten at the book club meeting?"

After retelling the story and talking about ideas for solving it, the kids set about working on the problem. Nafeesa used her ten fingers to help her solve the problem, using fingers up and fingers down to represent the number of chocolate and lemon cupcakes. Ronaldo used yellow and brown Unifix cubes, counting out ten yellow cubes for his first combination and ten chocolate ones for his second combination. After these two combinations, Ronaldo stopped, seemingly satisfied that he had solved the problem. Berto knew that five and five is ten, so he immediately recorded this with a drawing on his paper, but then seemed at a loss as to what to do next. Marisol began with ten brown Unifix cubes to represent ten chocolate cupcakes. She then systematically began removing one brown cube and replacing it with a yellow cube and recording the new combination.

"Let's take a little break to chat for a minute. You guys have some great thoughts to share, but I think some of you might be stuck too. When you were thinking about this problem, some combinations were easy for you. You thought of them right away. Which combinations did you think of first?"

"I already know that five plus five is ten," said Berto, proudly pointing to the drawing on his paper of five chocolate cupcakes and five yellow cupcakes.

"I made ten chocolate cupcakes because I love chocolate!" Ronaldo said.

After recording these ideas, I returned to our mathematician statement. "We know that mathematicians look for many ways to take numbers apart and put them together. Sometimes this can be tricky though. We *think* there are more ways to make ten, but we're not sure how to figure them out. How can we use the idea that mathematicians look for many ways to take numbers apart and put them together?"

"You can put some fingers up, like maybe six," explained Nafeesa, lifting six fingers. "So then you can say that's six chocolate cupcakes, and one, two, three, four are lemon cupcakes," Nafeesa continued, counting the four fingers that remained lowered on her hands.

"You can start with all brown cubes," explained Marisol. "Then if I take away one brown cube I have to add one yellow cube so it's still ten cubes. If I take away two brown cubes I have to add two yellow cubes. It's like I take the ten apart when I take brown cubes away and then I put it back together when I put in the yellow cubes."

After highlighting Nafeesa's connection to looking for combinations with her raised and lowered fingers and Marisol's more systematic compensation strategy (taking x brown cubes away and replacing them with x yellow cubes), and after asking Berto and Ronaldo to paraphrase these strategies, we went back to problem solving. "It sounds like you have a few ideas for *how* mathematicians take numbers apart and put them together," I said. "Try one of these ideas to see if you can find another way to make ten cupcakes."

The use of the mathematician statement not only helped me explain a practice of mathematicians—something they do—but also provided an opportunity for me to facilitate and focus a reflection on *how* it is that mathematicians are able to accomplish this important practice. Mathematician statements can help slow down thinking so that we can encourage children to be more reflective.

Another teaching practice for slowing down to go deeper in our thinking is to explicitly notice mathematical behaviors and practices. Take a look at these teacher statements:

- *I noticed you changed your mind about how to solve this problem and you are trying a different way. That's what mathematicians do.*
- *I noticed you started out* (name strategy or tool used) *and now you're* (name new strategy or tool). *What happened?*

- *I noticed you got out a pile of five cubes and a pile of twelve cubes. Now you seem stuck. Tell me about that.*
- *I noticed you found your mistake and fixed it. That's what mathematicians do.*
- *I noticed you* (mathematician statement). *That's what mathematicians do.*
- *I noticed you used to* (name less sophisticated strategy) *and now you* (name more sophisticated strategy). *Why do you think that is?*

This explicit noticing of student mathematical practices and behaviors serves two purposes:

1. It makes the thinking and actions of the child visible. The child may not be metacognitively aware or be able to articulate what he or she is doing. These statements end in the affirming language, "That's what mathematicians do."
2. It pushes the child to reexamine his or her thinking, with the goal of revising or simply being able to articulate thinking. These statements end in questioning language like, "Why do you think that is?"

Recently I was working with a group of three kindergartners on a rather tricky Compare Difference Unknown problem:

Caroline has 8 gummy bears. Her brother, Ricky, has 4 gummy bears. How many more gummy bears does Caroline have than Ricky?

Caroline and Ali were struggling with the problem. "You *told* us," said Ali, exasperated. "Caroline has eight gummy bears."

"Yeah, eight is the answer," confirmed Caroline.

As Caroline, Ali, and I worked through making sense of the problem, Marcos immediately began arranging two carefully constructed lines with teddy bear counters (see Figure 8.1). After making one line of four teddy bear counters and another line of eight, Marcos put his pencil across the two lines and counted the extra bears in the line of eight. Noticing that Marcos was using a modeling strategy common to Compare Difference Unknown strategy, I wanted to slow down the conversation and focus the students on understanding exactly what Marcos was doing.

"I notice that Marcos has a strategy. He's doing something really interesting with his lines of bears. What do you notice about what Marcos is doing?" I asked Caroline and Ali.

"He's got lines," Caroline commented.

Figure 8.1 Marcos created two lines of teddy bears to solve the Compare Difference Unknown problem.

"And what do you notice about these lines?" I asked.

"There's four bears here for Caroline's brother, Ricky, and eight bears here for Caroline. I told you the answer was eight!" explained Ali, still frustrated with me for presenting a problem that, to him, seemed to require no solving at all.

"But I also notice that Marcos put his pencil here, after the fourth bear in each line. Why did you do that, Marcos?"

"'Cause that's how I tell where the *more* is. See, it's one, two, three, four more," explained Marcos.

"So, let's listen to the story again and see if we can figure what's happening from what Marcos built," I said to the group.

By using noticing language myself and asking children to do the same, I helped the math exchange group members see each other as resources. Caroline and Ali might not internalize the structure of Compare Difference Unknown problems through this single exchange, but with continued reflective practice they will be able to fully take advantage of the collaborative power of the math exchange and achieve more than they could on their own or through interaction with the teacher alone.

Being a reflective learner often involves slowing down our thinking and really analyzing what is behind what we are doing. This doesn't come naturally for most people, and thus involves deliberate practice and teacher facilitation. It is worth the effort, though. Once you establish a culture of reflection in which deep thinking is valued, students will adopt this practice in mathematics and throughout their day.

Teaching for Self-Monitoring

Ellin Keene and Susan Zimmermann write about self-monitoring as "the umbrella under which other comprehension strategies fall" (2007, 49). Even though Keene and Zimmermann write specifically about reading comprehension strategies, the same is true of mathematics comprehension. As these authors point out, we should teach self-monitoring in a way that "emphasizes the importance of revising our thinking as we read, being metacognitive, and paying attention so that we know when we're understanding and when we're not and can do something about it" (49).

My work with Annabelle, a second grader, always reminded me of the importance of being explicit when teaching self-monitoring skills. Annabelle was a child with a learning disability; she had difficulty recognizing and recalling patterns and numbers as well as difficulty interpreting the structure of story problems. She struggled when counting, pausing before every change to a new decade to try to remember what the next number is called. When reading a number she often guessed a random number and waited to be told the correct number. When solving story problems Annabelle asked, "So I put together or I take apart?" and waited for an adult or classmate to elaborate with further direction.

While internalizing and recalling patterns and structures may have been particularly difficult for Annabelle because of her learning disability, her lack of self-monitoring and her use of random guessing at the point of difficulty was most concerning to me.

One day I sat down on the carpet with Annabelle, Shelton, Jorge, and Montana for a math exchange. Before starting our story problem, I wanted to get them warmed up saying and ordering numbers within the same range that we would be using when we problem solved. "Let's start with a mini-counting circle with the five of us," I said. "We'll start at twenty-five and count by ones. Can you start for us, Montana?" The count went smoothly until Shelton said twenty-nine and looked expectantly at Annabelle.

"Ninety?" Annabelle guessed. Annabelle had learned from previous classroom and home experiences that guessing any decade number would often result in a teacher, parent, or classmate jumping in with the correct number. Unfortunately, this strategy was not helping Annabelle self-monitor her own learning.

"That's a guess, Annabelle," I said warmly, but firmly. "What can you do when you're not sure what number comes next?"

"Use a number chart?" Annabelle responded, unsure of herself.

"Yes, that's one thing you can do. Show us how you can use the number chart to help you figure out what number comes next."

Annabelle picked up a number chart, began at 1, and ran her fingers across the numbers, whispering the count until she found 29. She backed up to 20 and began again. "Twenty, 21, 22, 23, 24, 25, 26, 27, 28, 29 . . . 30! It's 30."

"Good job, Annabelle! You used a strategy to figure out what the next number would be when you didn't know. That's what mathematicians do." Even though Annabelle had to go through a fairly arduous task to figure out that thirty comes after twenty-nine, it was important for me to reinforce that when she was aware that she didn't know something, she could do things on her own to figure it out.

Pat Johnson (2006) describes this process for readers in a way that makes a lot of sense for mathematics as well: "Being a problem solver means actively initiating the use of strategies. Proficient readers *take action* when they become stuck; they use multiple strategies at the point of difficulty" (28). Learning to connect the words, symbols, and quantities of math is more difficult for some children than for others. It is tempting to give too much support to these children because it is difficult to watch them struggling with what seems like a very basic task. However, the best thing we can do for struggling and soaring mathematicians alike is give them tools for monitoring their understanding and strategies for problem solving.

Sometimes self-monitoring for understanding takes the form of something similar to what Annabelle did—using a strategy at the point of difficulty to help herself figure something out. Other times helping children create an awareness of understanding and misunderstanding is the place to start. I like to make an analogy to a common reading experience when talking about how I, an adult reader and mathematician, monitor my understanding. For example, when meeting with one group of students, I said, "Yesterday I was reading an article about how different animals communicate with each other. I was really interested in the article—that's why I picked it up in the first place—but after about five minutes of reading I realized I hadn't understood anything I had just read. Sure, I had read all of the words, but I didn't understand what the author was trying to say about animals communicating with each other. Has that ever happened to you when you read?" Students shared experiences of being confused or "not getting it" when they read. This is a common experience for all readers, and I lowered the risk involved in sharing by telling them of my own experience.

I went on to explain, "Your brain is doing something important when you realize that you haven't understood that last three pages you've read. It's yelling, 'Stop! What you're doing isn't working.' When I was reading that article and I realized my brain was saying, 'Stop!' I said to myself, 'I'm not getting this. Do I want to understand this? If I do, I need to go back and read it again. I need to think more about what the scientists are saying and check often to make sure I'm understanding.'"

We'd talked about this before within the realm of reading. Now I wanted to make the connection to math. "I've told you about the grown-up math classes I take sometimes where I work on problems that are hard for me," I said. "Sometimes I look at a problem and think, 'Maybe I should know how to do this, maybe the teacher thinks I should be able to do this, but I have no idea what this problem means.' Just realizing this is important. Because then I can decide what I want to do. Do I want to ask the teacher for help? Do I want to see if a friend can help me? Do I want to try it on my own and see how far I can get? I have choices, but just realizing that I don't understand is the first step—and it's really important. Today I'm going to give you some challenging problems to work on—you might not always understand them, and that's okay. But I want you to think about when you understand and when you don't understand. That's your important job to do as we work today."

Math exchanges are a great place to help students create greater awareness of their own thinking and understanding. The small-group format allows many children to take risks and open up to the group about their own understanding and misunderstanding. A whole-group setting is sometimes too intimidating, so children hide their misunderstanding with silence.

Working with third graders Randy, Eva, Eugene, and Wilbert provided me with an opportunity to see the power of teaching self-monitoring through math exchanges. Randy was a student who doubted himself constantly. "I'm *not* a mathematician," he cried defiantly whenever we reflected on mathematician statements. He refused to take on the identity of mathematician for fear of failure in this role. Wilbert, though a fairly confident mathematician, did not self-monitor for understanding. Wilbert shared after one math exchange, "One hundred three minus ten is thirteen." There were no alarm bells going off in his head that asked, "Does it make sense? Does that seem about right?" Eugene and Eva were both excellent explainers of their thinking. They knew when things didn't make sense and when they did, and although Eugene was a stronger math student than Eva, Eva's ability to realize when she understood something and when she needed to figure out a way to help herself understand set her apart from the others in the group.

In thinking about guiding this group, I knew I wanted to focus on self-monitoring for understanding. I wanted them, independently, to be able to realize when they were understanding and when they were not understanding. I wanted them to be able to ask questions to clarify their understanding and eventually advocate for themselves as learners. I had goals for each of these students mathematically, but I knew they could not be fully successful in their mathematics until they were self-monitoring their understanding.

As I sat down with this group I told them the purpose of our work in this math exchange. "Today we are going to work on a problem, and I want you to think about what and when you understand and when you are confused or not really sure what to do." I read a story problem to them. "We went to Huntley Meadows wetland on a field trip. We found all sorts of insects—141 in total. Seventy-three were ants and the rest were crickets, butterflies, grasshoppers, and beetles. We also saw robins building nests to lay their eggs. We learned that robins usually lay about three eggs at a time. Everyone in our classroom came on the field trip, except Meg and Randy, who were sick with the flu."

I took a deep breath. "Phew! I just gave you a lot of information. Sometimes you probably understood what I was telling you and were thinking of questions I would ask you, and other times a little voice in your head may have been thinking, 'What in the world is going on?' Tell me what the little voices were saying in your brain."

Eva was first to pipe up. "I kept waiting for you to ask a question! When you said we saw 141 insects and 73 were ants, I thought you were going ask how many were some other bug."

"I thought that too!" said Eugene.

"Well, could I ask you that?" I said.

"Yeah," said Wilbert. "It's just 141 minus 73. You could subtract or you could add up from 73."

"No, you can't!" said Randy, slightly rudely. Randy is much more comfortable with the misunderstandings of others than with his own.

"Why not?" I asked.

"There are too many animals. It's a big mess," responded Randy in his typical matter-of-fact way.

"So, Randy, when you were listening to me telling the story something in your brain told you, 'There's something not quite right here.' Let's listen again, and I want you all to figure out what it is that made Randy realize this."

I read the beginning of the story again.

"I don't get it. How can you figure out anything else when there are crickets, butterflies, grasshoppers, and beetles?" wondered Eva.

"You *can't* figure it out. If it just said, 'We found 141 insects, 73 were ants, and the rest were crickets,' we could figure it out. But we don't know how many were crickets, how many were butterflies, how many were grasshoppers, and how many were beetles," explained Eugene.

"So," I pointed out, "something in your brain told you, 'There's something not quite right here; let me take a closer look.' Let's practice listening to that voice. I'm going to read the second part of the story to you again."

As we continued working through the story, the kids practiced activating the little voice in their heads that checks for understanding. Teaching children to be aware of their thinking and to expand it to help them problem solve is a valuable skill.

Utilizing this skill will, for example, help the child's internal alarm go off when she subtracts 19 from 150 and gets an answer of 149. She will think, "That answer is way too big. I subtracted a lot, so there can't possibly still be 149 left." Awareness of our own thinking will also promote the use of self-talk to work through difficulty: "This problem seems impossible. It's really frustrating me. I've done hard problems before though, so maybe if I skip it and come back to it, I'll think of a way to do it." These are skills we, as adults, have mostly likely learned through a lot of trial and error. Children can also learn these skills with guidance and practice.

Content Reflection and Process Reflection

I strive to achieve balance between two kinds of reflection during math workshop: content reflection, as seen in the preceding math exchange about insects, and process reflection. Content reflection focuses on a specific math concept or strategy that you and your class have been discussing and working on. After several sessions of counting collections (see Chapter 6 for a discussion of counting collections), I noticed that many of my second graders were exploring the idea of grouping by fives and tens in order to organize and more efficiently count a collection of objects. I asked a few of these students if they would bring their math journals to the rug to share how they had been counting. Jocelyn held up her notebook for the class to see as we gathered on the rug at the end of math workshop. "I counted tiny animal erasers," she said. "There were a lot of them! I counted out groups of ten. Then I counted those groups. Ten, 20, 30, 40, 50, 60. And then I counted the extras that weren't a group of ten. Sixty-one, 62, 63."

"What did you understand about how Jocelyn counted the erasers?" I asked the class, looking for children to restate and rephrase her idea. José shared his strategy next.

"I counted the Lego pieces by fives. Five, 10, 15, 20, 25, 30, 35, 40, 45, 50, 55, 56, 57, 58. There are 58 Legos. Those ones after 55 are the extras that didn't make a group."

"So, what do you all notice about how Jocelyn and José organized and made groups to make counting easier?" I asked. Students rephrased what they had heard Jocelyn and José explain about grouping objects in order to count more efficiently, the math concept I wanted them to focus on.

Process reflection on the other hand, focuses on developing the practices and behaviors of a strong mathematician. "Mathematicians talk with other mathematicians about what is difficult and try to problem solve together." This is a simple statement, but anyone who has ever taught knows that expressing what is difficult in a problem and working collaboratively toward a common goal is a skill that must be taught, practiced, and refined. In my classroom much of this rich process reflective discussion comes from the mathematician statements my students and I write together.

How I've Changed as a Mathematician: Students' Reflective Projects

About halfway through the year, I ask my students to spend some time looking through their problem-solving notebooks. I ask them, "What do you remember about the problems we've solved this year? Did you have a favorite story problem? Which ones were tricky? Now that you're a little older and a stronger mathematician, do you think you'd solve any of the problems differently than you did before?" Looking back at the work they have done earlier in the year always creates a sense of pride in my young mathematicians' hearts. They can't believe they have solved so many problems! And since they are now much older and wiser than they were in September, they are eager to point out that they now know much more efficient ways to solve the problems they worked on earlier in the year.

"Look, Ms. Wedekind!" Alejandra says, waving a piece of paper in front of me. "Do you remember when I didn't know that you could count by tens from thirty-four? I had to count all the way from thirty-four to seventy-nine by ones on the hundreds grid. I can't believe it!"

"And how would you solve that problem now that you've changed as a mathematician, Alejandra?"

"Easy! Thirty-four, 44, 54, 64, 74. That's 40. Seventy-five, 76, 77, 78, 79. That's 5. So 45."

"You *have* changed, Alejandra. Knowing how to make jumps of ten has really helped you grow as a mathematician," I say, thrilled, not just for Alejandra's deeper understanding of numbers and more efficient strategies, but for the self-awareness she has of herself as a mathematician.

As our math workshop starts to wind up, I ask the kids to choose one problem they would solve differently now and bring it to the circle. As we share our problems during the reflection time, I hear kids talking about new strategies and understandings and mathematical misconceptions that they have cleared up in their minds. I also hear them say things like, "When I was little at the beginning of third grade, I used to get frustrated if I couldn't figure something out in a snap. Now I'm patient and persistent." I want to stand up and shout, "Yes!" All of those mathematician statements and language I have introduced have been taken on and owned by the kids. They really are much smarter and wiser than they were in September.

The next day I bring blank copies of the story problems that the kids talked about in our last math workshop. "I want you to solve this problem in the different way you told us about yesterday. Then we're going to make charts and posters about how we've changed as mathematicians. Let me show you my chart."

At the top of a sheet of chart paper I have written, "How I've Changed as a Mathematician." I look at the notes I jotted down on a sticky note the night before. At first I had trouble thinking about how I would model mathematical change in myself as an adult in a way that would mirror what is occurring for my students as child mathematicians, but I came up with a plan that I think will work and I start to create my chart so the whole class can see. I draw a line down the middle of my paper and label the sides "Before" and "Now." On the "Before" side I start with a picture of myself that I've drawn for my kids on other occasions to show them what stressed out or anxious feels like for me. It's me as a stick figure with big round eyes and crazy brown hair sticking straight up. I draw a speech bubble above the crazy hair and write, "Aaah!" in it. As I draw the stressed-out Kassia, I tell my kids that I used to feel this way when I saw that something in math was really hard for my students. I used to panic, "Oh, no! They're never going to understand! I have to tell them how to do it!" Then I draw an arrow across to the "Now" side of my paper. I draw a much more peaceful Kassia—with hair in order and a big smile. "This is hard for the kids, but it's going to be okay," I write in the speech bubble. "I know how to help them figure it out." I tell my kids that, just like them, I had to learn to be patient and persistent and had to learn to try new strategies when old ones weren't working anymore. This is a process reflection, something I want to encourage my kids to reflect upon (although I don't name it as such for them). I simply say, "I'm drawing and writing about how my feelings and thoughts about being a mathematician have changed."

Next I chart my learning of mathematics content. In planning my chart the night before, I knew I wanted to write something genuine, but something that they would be able to understand. My kids are used to me telling them about the "grown-up math classes" I go to—the math professional development I attend. So I say, "In my math class this year I learned a lot about thinking about fractions and decimals on a number line. Before, I thought of fractions as pieces of a pizza or sharing cookies or the part of the class that wears glasses." I record these ideas in the "Before" section of my chart. "Now when I think about fractions," I continue, drawing and writing in the "Now" section of my chart, "I'm often comparing them to other fractions using a number line, just like you guys do in here." I add a few more notes about myself as a mathematician. It is important for them to see me as a learner modeling my own reflective thinking. "Now I want you to work on your own charts about how you have changed as a mathematician. You'll be showing how you solve the problem you chose differently now than you did earlier in the year. You'll also add other information about how you've grown and changed as a mathematician."

The first time I worked on this project with my second and third graders, I was not sure what to expect. Would they be capable of this kind of metacognitive thinking? I could not have been more pleasantly surprised.

The strategies they used to re-solve problems they had solved in September truly demonstrated a shift in thinking. Second grader Martín chose to reflect on this problem:

> Amber is walking along the river with some stones in her pocket. She picks up 39 more rocks on her walk. When she gets home she has 75 stones. How many stones did she start with in her pocket?

I remember when Martín first solved this Join Start Unknown problem. He had a hard time figuring out what was going on in the story and for what he needed to solve. After conversations with classmates and with me he eventually used a hundreds grid to count the spaces between 39 and 75. Now, later in the year, he had a strategy that revealed a greater understanding of how numbers work. Martín wrote:

$$39 + 1 = 40$$
$$40 + 30 = 70$$
$$70 + 5 = 75$$
$$30 + 5 + 1 = 36$$

Figure 8.2 These students create How I've Changed as a Mathematician projects in Spanish, the language in which they received math instruction.

The students' math wasn't the only impressive part of their How I've Changed as a Mathematician projects. They wrote about peace, persistence, patience, and taking a break to gather your thoughts when something is really hard. They drew pictures of themselves thinking, solving problems with big proud smiles on their faces, and finding ways to mathematize the world around them (see Figure 8.2). The opportunity to reflect upon and recognize how they had grown was a powerful process for these kids.

Becoming a Reflective Teacher

In order to promote a culture of reflection in our classrooms, we must be reflective teachers. A colleague of mine whom I very much respect once told me that she believed that devoting thirty minutes daily to thinking, reading, and writing with the purpose of reflection was key to good teaching. This colleague told me, "Kassia, you can't be a good teacher if you're just racing ahead at full speed from one day to the next without stopping to consider if what you are doing is working for the kids and for you. You'll be a very busy teacher, but you won't be a very good one." Such true words! In my continuing effort to become a more reflective teacher, I have started noticing what it is that reflective teachers I so admire do. I have come up with the following list, which I continually add to, and have put these ideas into practice in my own teaching life.

Practices of Reflective Teachers

- Journal about your teaching life. Write about what your teaching feels like, what you're struggling with, what is going really well, and powerful things kids say.
- Find a reflection partner. My teaching friend Katie and I meet for an early breakfast once a week before school. We share ideas and projects we are working on with our classes; we talk about new books and plan getaways to conferences. By the time we walk through the school doors at 8:15 with our iced teas in hand, I feel relaxed and ready to start the day. The time I lose in morning planning is made up in the feeling of anticipation and excitement about sharing a love for teaching. Find your own reflection partner and together over coffee chat about a new idea or a practice about which you are wondering. Make sure these reflection sessions don't turn into gripe sessions. Sometimes it feels good to get a frustration off your chest, but dwelling too long in that place will only make you feel zapped of energy rather than reenergized.
- Join a teachers-as-readers group. Or start one yourself! Grab your favorite pen and some sticky notes (I'm an office supply nut), and share your love of professional books with other colleagues.
- Become a member of a professional group and take time to read their monthly publication.

Living a Rich Mathematical Life

Regie Routman (2008) writes about the importance of living a life full of experiences that we can take back into the classroom to share with our students. One particular story Routman tells in *Teaching Essentials* hit home with me one year in the late fall when I was feeling overwhelmed and not wholly satisfied with my teaching. Routman writes, "One of the things I love best in the summer is to make fruit pies and tarts. When the berries in the Northwest are luscious and the stone fruits are beautifully ripe, I create all kinds of delicious and gorgeous desserts. It's sheer fun" (2008, 129). When I first read this, I snapped the book shut. "How does this woman have time for berry picking with all the teaching and writing she does? Why can't I do that too?" I demanded. I opened the book again to reread and found this sentence: "I am a more interesting person if I have stories to tell that are not just about school" (127). I pondered this thought and asked myself, "How can I teach my students to live a rich, full life inside and outside of the classroom if I am not doing this myself?"

And so I set out to live a rich life, specifically a rich mathematical life that would provide me with stories, experiences, and questions to draw from when teaching. I started riding my bike more often. I spent afternoons going on walks with friends and taking the metro into Washington, D.C., to explore museums. As a math teacher, I tend to see the world through my math lenses. I decided that, like Regie Routman, I would use my rich mathematical life as a springboard for mathematical storytelling in my classroom.

I took pictures wherever I went. I took pictures of a pigeon who decided to make a nest on the flower planter on my balcony. I brought the pictures into my class with me. After the bird laid her eggs I wondered aloud with my students how long it would be until the eggs hatched. We looked it up on the Internet and constructed a number line counting back from 17 days, the number of days in which we expected the baby pigeon to hatch. Every day my students would come up to me and ask, "Are the eggs still there? Have they hatched?"

"They're still there, and they haven't hatched yet," I replied. "Let's see how many more days until we think they'll hatch," I encouraged, pointing to our number line.

In the winter of 2009–2010, Washington, D.C., experienced the two biggest snowstorms we have had in the past century. During the first storm, I trekked out in the snow with my husband for long, snowy walks, wrapped up in layers upon layers of warm clothes we rarely use. We measured the snow each hour, and again I took pictures. When we all finally returned to school I showed my kids the pictures and told them the stories of how much it snowed. Luckily for us there was to be another giant storm that winter. Many of the kids measured the snowfall at their homes and were eager to tell stories of their own rich mathematical lives when we returned to school: "When I woke up there were already 8 inches of snow! And then when I measured again that night we were up to 14 inches!"

Mathematics is everywhere if you are out there and open to it (and even sometimes when you're not). It's the hexagon pattern of the tiles in the metro station near my house, the towering display of toilet paper at my grocery store

(*How many packs are there in that display? How many rolls are there?*), and the happy hour sushi specials on my Friday night dates with my husband (*$3.99 for a spicy tuna roll, regularly $5.99. How much money am I saving?*).

Live a rich mathematical life, and share this life with your students. Help them to create a life rich in joyful mathematical experiences. Tell stories together. Become empowered mathematicians and empower others to do the same.

Math Exchange Note-Taking Sheet

Week of _____

Group:
Focus/Plan

Group:
Focus/Plan

Group:
Focus/Plan

Group:
Focus/Plan

Group:
Focus/Plan

Group:
Focus/Plan

Notes on Work of Individual Children		
	Notes:	

Join Problems

Join Result Unknown (JRU)	Join Change Unknown (JCU)	Join Start Unknown (JSU)
Eva had 5 cookies. Antonio gave her 10 more cookies. How many cookies does Eva have altogether/in all/in total/now?	Eva has 5 cookies. How many more cookies does she need to have 15 cookies?	Eva had some cookies. Antonio gave her 10 more cookies. Now she has 15 cookies. How many cookies did Eva have to start with?

Separate Problems

Separate Result Unknown (SRU)	Separate Change Unknown (SCU)	Separate Start Unknown (SSU)
Eva had 15 cookies. She gave 5 cookies to Antonio. How many cookies does she have left/now?	Eva had 15 cookies. She gave some to Antonio. Now she has 5 cookies left. How many cookies did she give to Antonio?	Eva had some cookies. She gave 5 to Antonio. Now she has 10 cookies left. How many cookies did Eva have to start with?

Part-Part-Whole Problems

Part-Part-Whole, with the Whole Unknown (PPWWU)	Part-Part-Whole, with One Part Unknown (PPWPU)
Eva has 5 lemon cookies and 10 chocolate cookies. How many cookies does Eva have?	Eva has 15 cookies. Five are lemon and the rest/the others are chocolate. How many chocolate cookies does Eva have?

Compare Problems

Compare Difference Unknown (CDU)	Compare Quantity Unknown (CQU)	Compare Referent Unknown (CRU)
Eva has 15 cookies. Antonio has 5 cookies. How many more cookies does Eva have than Antonio?	Antonio has 5 cookies. Eva has 10 more cookies than Antonio. How many cookies does Eva have?	Eva has 15 cookies. She has 10 more cookies than Antonio. How many cookies does Antonio have?

Multiplication and Division Problems

Multiplication	Measurement Division	Partitive Division
Eva has 3 plates. She puts 5 cookies on each plate. How many cookies does Eva have?	Eva has 15 cookies. She wants to put 5 cookies on each plate. How many plates will Eva need?	Antonio has 15 cookies. He wants to put the same number of cookies on 3 plates. How many cookies can Antonio put on each plate?

Adapted from Carpenter et al. 1999.

Math Exchanges—A Month at a Glance

Month _____

Student's Name	Week 1 Dates:	Week 2 Dates:	Week 3 Dates:	Week 4 Dates:

Calendar of Math Exchanges

Month _____

Monday	Tuesday	Wednesday	Thursday	Friday

Analyzing Student Work, Thinking, and Understanding

Name and Grade: _____ Date: _____

Evidence of Student Thinking	What Can the Student Do?	What Can the Student Almost Do/Not Yet Do?	Next Steps
Noticing ⟶	Interpreting ⟶		Responding
			How Will I Know?

References

Atwell, Nancie. 1998. *In the Middle: Writing, Reading, and Learning with Adolescents.* 2nd ed. Portsmouth, NH: Heinemann.

Bohm, David. 1996. *On Dialogue.* New York: Routledge Classics.

Buschman, Larry. 2003. "Children Who Enjoy Problem Solving." *Teaching Children Mathematics* 9 (9): 539–544.

Calkins, Lucy. 1994. *The Art of Teaching Writing.* New ed. Portsmouth, NH: Heinemann.

Carpenter, Thomas P., Elizabeth Fennema, Megan Loef Franke, and Linda Levi. 1999. *Children's Mathematics: Cognitively Guided Instruction.* Portsmouth, NH: Heinemann.

Common Core State Standards Initiative. 2010. "Mathematics: Kindergarten: Introduction." Common Core State Standards Initiative. http://www.corestandards.org/the-standards/mathematics/kindergarten/introduction/.

Devlin, Keith. 2000. *The Math Gene: How Mathematical Thinking Evolved and Why Numbers Are Like Gossip.* New York: Basic Books.

———. 2005. *The Math Instinct: Why You're a Mathematical Genius (Along with Lobsters, Birds, Cats, and Dogs).* New York: Thunder's Mouth Press.

Fosnot, Catherine Twomey. 2005. *Constructivism: Theory, Perspectives, and Practice.* 2nd ed. New York: Teachers College Press.

Fosnot, Catherine Twomey, and Maarten Dolk. 2001. *Young Mathematicians at Work: Constructing Number Sense, Addition, and Subtraction.* Portsmouth, NH: Heinemann.

Fuson, Karen C., Douglas H. Clements, and Sybilla Beckmann. 2010. *Focus in Kindergarten: Teaching with Curriculum Focal Points.* Reston, VA: National Council of Teachers of Mathematics.

Hyde, Arthur. 2006. *Comprehending Math: Adapting Reading Strategies to Teach Mathematics K–6.* Portsmouth, NH: Heinemann.

Johnson, Pat. 2006. *One Child at a Time: Making the Most of Your Time with Struggling Readers, K–6.* Portland, ME: Stenhouse.

Johnston, Peter H. 2004. *Choice Words: How Our Language Affects Children's Learning.* Portland, ME: Stenhouse.

Jung, M. W., P. Kloosterman, and M. B. McMullen. 2007. "Young Children's Natural Intuition for Number and Problem Solving: A Research in Review." *Young Children* 62 (5): 50–57.

Kamii, Constance. 1994. *Young Children Continue to Reinvent Arithmetic, 3rd Grade: Implications of Piaget's Theory.* New York: Teachers College Press.

———. 2000. *Young Children Reinvent Arithmetic: Implications of Piaget's Theory.* 2nd ed. New York: Teachers College Press.

Keene, Ellin Oliver. 2008. *To Understand: New Horizons in Reading Comprehension.* Portsmouth, NH: Heinemann.

Keene, Ellin Oliver, and Susan Zimmermann. 2007. *Mosaic of Thought: The Power of Comprehension Strategy Instruction.* 2nd ed. Portsmouth, NH: Heinemann.

Litwin, Eric. 2010. *Pete the Cat: I Love My White Shoes.* New York: HarperCollins.

Miller, Debbie. 2008. *Teaching with Intention: Defining Beliefs, Aligning Practice, Taking Action.* Portland, ME: Stenhouse.

Muth, Jon. 2002. *The Three Questions.* New York: Scholastic Press.

NCTM (National Council of Teachers of Mathematics). 2011a. "Process Standards." NCTM. http://www.nctm.org/standards/content.aspx?id=322.

———. 2011b. "Welcome to the Curriculum Focal Points." NCTM. http://www.nctm.org/standards/content.aspx?id=3514.

———. 2011c. "Number and Operations." *Principles and Standards for School Mathematics.* http://www.nctm.org/standards/content.aspx?id=7564.

Nichols, Maria. 2006. *Comprehension Through Conversation: The Power of Purposeful Talk in the Reading Workshop.* Portsmouth, NH: Heinemann.

Novakowski, Janice. 2007. "Developing 'Five-ness' in Kindergarten." *Teaching Children Mathematics* 14 (4): 226–231.

Outhred, Lynne, and Sarah Sardelich. 2005. "'A Problem Is Something You Don't Want to Have': Problem Solving by Kindergarteners." *Teaching Children Mathematics*. 12 (3): 146–154.

Richardson, Kathy. 1998. *Developing Number Concepts, Book 3: Place Value, Multiplication, and Division*. White Plains, NY: Dale Seymour.

Ross, Sharon. 1986. "The Development of Children's Place-Value Numeration Concepts in Grades Two Through Five." Paper presented at the annual meeting of the American Educational Research Association, San Francisco, April 16–20.

———. 1990. "Children's Acquisition of Place-Value Numeration Concepts: The Roles of Cognitive Development and Instruction." *Focus on Learning Problems in Mathematics* 12 (1): 1–17.

Routman, Regie. 2008. *Teaching Essentials: Expecting the Most and Getting the Best from Every Learner, K–8*. Portsmouth, NH: Heinemann.

Schwerdtfeger, Julie Kern, and Angela Chan. 2007. "Counting Collections." *Teaching Children Mathematics* 13 (7): 356–361.

Steinbeck, John. 1994 [1937]. *Of Mice and Men*. New York: Penguin.

TERC. 2008. *Investigations in Number, Data, and Space*. Cambridge, MA: Pearson Education.

U.S. National Research Center. 1996. *Summary of Eighth Grade Curriculum Results*. U.S. National Research Center, Report No. 7: 5.

Van de Walle, John, and LouAnn Lovin. 2006. *Teaching Student-Centered Mathematics: Grades K–3*. Boston: Allyn and Bacon.

Wickett, Maryann, and Marilyn Burns. 2002. *Teaching Arithmetic: Lessons for Introducing Place Value, Grade 2*. Sausalito, CA: Math Solutions.

———. 2005. *Teaching Arithmetic: Lessons for Extending Place Value, Grade 3*. Sausalito, CA: Math Solutions.

Index

Math Exchanges

Guiding Young Mathematicians in Small-Group Meetings

Kassia Omohundro Wedekind

Foreword by Suzanne H. Chapin

Stenhouse Publishers • Portland, Maine

Stenhouse Publishers
www.stenhouse.com

Credits
The poem "Numbers" by Mary Cornish is from *Poetry* magazine, Volume CLXXVI, Number 3, June 2010. Copyright © 2000 by the Modern Poetry Association. All rights reserved.

Library of Congress Cataloging-in-Publication Data
Omohundro Wedekind, Kassia
    Math exchanges : guiding young mathematicians in small-group meetings / Kassia Omohundro Wedekind.
        p. cm.
    Includes bibliographical references and index.
    ISBN 978-1-57110-826-5 (pbk. : alk. paper) — ISBN 978-1-57110-923-1 (e-book) 1. Mathematics—Study and teaching (Elementary) 2. Mathematics—Study and teaching (Preschool) 3. Group guidance in education. I. Title.
    QA20.G76W43 2011
    372.7'044—dc23

                                                                    2011014818

Cover design, interior design, and typesetting by Martha Drury

Manufactured in the United States of America

PRINTED ON 30% PCW
    RECYCLED PAPER

22 21 20 19 18   10 9 8 7 6